CHILD'S
BIBLE

IN COLOUR

The Old Testament

First published in Great Britain in 1969
and distributed by Wolfe Publishing Ltd.

First published in the U.S.A. in 1978 by Paulist Press
Editorial Office: 1865 Broadway, New York, N.Y. 10023
Business Office: 545 Island Road, Ramsey, N.J. 07446

Library of Congress
Catalog Card Number: 78-51444
ISBN: 0-8091-2117-4

Printed and bound in the
United States of America

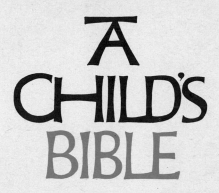

A CHILD'S BIBLE

IN COLOUR

The Old Testament

Re-written for children by
ANNE EDWARDS

Illustrated by
CHARLES FRONT and DAVID CHRISTIAN

PAULIST PRESS
New York, N.Y./Ramsey, N.J./Toronto

R. RAMSES

EGYPT

CONTENTS

GENESIS

THE FIRST SEVEN DAYS

GENESIS 1

A very long time ago there was no heaven and no earth and no darkness and no light and so God said, "Let there be light," and there was! And He called the light, day . . . and the darkness, night. And that was the first day.

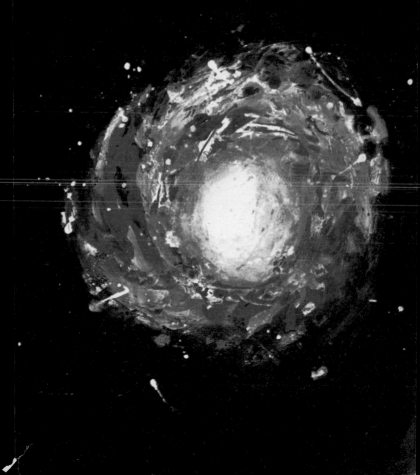

But when the light came up on the second day, God could see that His work was not done and so He said, "Let there be a sky," and there was a sky!

On the third day God could see He *still* had more work to do and so He created the dry land which He called the earth and the water which He called the seas, and very quickly there were grass and plants and trees with lovely fruits.

On the fourth day God added to the sky the sun and the stars so that there would *always* be light.

And on the fifth day there was so much beauty that God added living things to make it *really* complete and so He created great whales and small fish and birds that could fly above the green trees and the rich earth and the deep blue seas.

God could see all this was good and beautiful and so on the sixth day He added every kind of animal —and then He created man!

By the seventh day God was tired from all this work, so He rested and blessed the seventh day and made it a day for all living things to rest.

And then when God had rested long enough He planted a garden eastward in a place called Eden and there He put the man whom He had made.

THE GARDEN OF EDEN

GENESIS 2

The Garden of Eden had every tree that was pleasant to behold and which bore good fruit to eat. But God planted two other trees in the Garden of Eden, one was the Tree of Life and the other was the Tree of Good and Evil, and when the Lord God put the man in the Garden of Eden He told him he was to care for the garden and for his work he could eat from any tree *except* from the Tree of Good and Evil—for if he ate from that he would surely die! And He called the man Adam but Adam—even with all the trees, the birds, and the animals—was lonely.

So one night while Adam slept God took one of Adam's ribs and from this rib He made a woman and when Adam woke the next morning God brought her to Adam and told him she would be called woman because part of her came from man. The woman became Adam's wife and Adam named his wife, Eve.

THE SERPENT

There was in the garden a serpent who was very evil and he asked Eve, "Did God forbid you to eat the fruit of the trees in the garden?"

"No," Eve answered, "we are only forbidden to eat the fruit on the tree in the middle of the garden. God said we would die if we did so."

"You will not die," the evil serpent told her.

And so Eve was tempted to eat the rich red fruit on the forbidden tree. And when she did she felt that indeed she was now very wise and so she gave Adam some of the fruit and he ate it.

Then they sewed fig leaves together to cover themselves as it was now the cool part of the day, and as they did they heard the voice of the Lord and because they knew they had done wrong they tried to hide from Him.

"Where are you?" the Lord God called.

And Adam stayed where he was because *he was ashamed.*

7

And the Lord God asked Adam, "Have you eaten the fruit I commanded you *not* to eat?"

"Eve gave it to me," Adam replied.

And the Lord God said to the woman: "What is this you have done?"

"The serpent tempted me," Eve told the Lord God, "and I ate."

The Lord God was very angry at the serpent and placed a curse on him: thereafter the serpent would have to crawl through life on his belly. Then the Lord God turned to Eve and told her that she would, from this time forth, be ruled by her husband and know great sorrow from her children. Then He told Adam he would have to work the land from whence he came to get his own food.

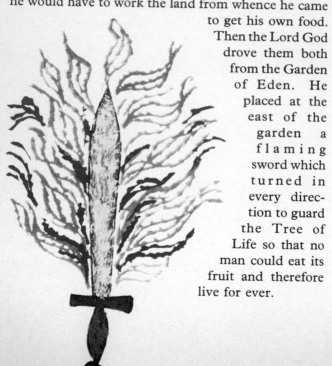

Then the Lord God drove them both from the Garden of Eden. He placed at the east of the garden a flaming sword which turned in every direction to guard the Tree of Life so that no man could eat its fruit and therefore live for ever.

CAIN AND ABEL

GENESIS 4-5

Adam and Eve did as the Lord God said and farmed the land and ate their own fruit and as time passed they had two sons, first Cain and then Abel.

Abel became a shepherd and Cain became a farmer, and when they both believed the time was right Cain offered some of his harvest to the Lord and Abel offered to the Lord his fattest and choicest of lambs. The Lord was very pleased with Abel's offering but He did not think Cain's was as good. Cain grew very angry at the Lord!

And God said to him, "Cain, why are you angry? If you do well with your land I will be pleased with your offering and if you do not do well I shall not be pleased."

But Cain refused to answer, and the anger grew so strong inside him that later, when both he and Abel were back in the fields together he struck Abel very hard and Abel did not get up!

The Lord God saw this and He called out, "Cain! What have you done? You have killed your own brother and for that you shall leave this place and never return.

Cain was frightened that if he were to wander in strange places unknown someone would try to kill him and the Lord God said to Cain, "Whosoever slays you shall have seven-fold your sorrow." Then He placed a mark upon Cain so that anyone finding him would know it was the Lord God's mark and would not kill him.

Cain then went to live in the land of Nod at the east of Eden. He wandered for many years. and then he married and his wife gave birth to a son they called Enoch and Cain built a city named after his son.

The Lord God then gave Eve and Adam another son and they called him Seth and they knew the Lord God now forgave them their past sins and so the earth began to grow into the many-peopled place it was to become.

But as the people multiplied *so did the evil they could seek.*

NOAH AND THE ARK

GENESIS 7

God saw that man was growing too wicked and He decided He would have to destroy all those He had created, man and beast and the creeping things and the birds. But there was one old man the Lord thought to spare and his name was Noah. Noah was a just man and so were his three sons—Shem, Ham and Japheth.

God said to Noah, "Make an ark of gopher wood, with rooms sealed inside and out with pitch. Make it three hundred feet long and fifty feet wide and three stories high with a small window and a door on the top and then into the ark bring your wife and your sons and your sons' wives and your grandchildren. And of every living thing bring two, a male and a female, and bring as well food for a long journey for all of you for as soon as your ark is finished and the last animal is on board and the door and the window are shut tight, I will bring a tremendous flood of waters upon the earth and everything that remains shall perish in it!"

THE FLOOD

GENESIS 7

Noah did as the Lord God told him. He went into the ark with his wife and his sons and his sons' wives and all his grandchildren and all the animals two by two. And as soon as the last animal was in the ark and the small window and the door were shut tight the Lord God caused it to rain for forty days and for forty nights and the ark was lifted by the waves above the earth and floated safely on the water.

THE FLOOD ENDS

God remembered Noah and every living thing with Noah in the ark and He made the waters go down again and there was no more rain, and Noah and the ark rested safely on the mountains of Ararat.

Then Noah sent out a raven which was not to return until the earth was dry and a dove which *was* to return if the waters were still upon the earth.

The dove came back and so Noah stayed in the ark another seven days. Then he sent the dove out again. He waited seven days and when the dove did not return he knew the earth was dry and behold! the earth *was* dry!

Noah left the ark with his wife and his sons and his sons' wives and his grandchildren and every animal, insect and bird, *everything* that lives today left the ark and went out on to the earth.

And the Lord God told Noah, "I will not curse the earth again; while the earth remains there will be seed-time and harvest-time and summer and winter and day and night."

THE RAINBOW

God blessed Noah and made a special vow that there would not be another flood to destroy the earth and as a token of that vow the Lord God said, "I set my rainbow in the cloud and it shall come to pass when I bring a cloud over the earth that the rainbow shall be seen in the cloud. I will look upon it and I will remember My vow to you and to every living creature on earth."

Many years passed and Noah's family grew and went forth to form nations.

THE TOWER OF BABEL

GENESIS 11

At this time all the people on earth spoke one language, and no matter how far they travelled they could understand each other. But, of course, they had only travelled over a small part of the earth. As they travelled eastward they finally grew tired and they settled in a land that they called Shinar. They decided to build a city and a tower in this city the very top of which would reach up to Heaven.

Everyone helped and soon the tower was climbing into the clouds and God came down to see what His children were doing. He was very upset! Heaven was a sacred place and could not be entered by building a tower. If this is what His children did when they understood each other then He would have to scatter the people of Babel all over the earth; changing each one's way of speaking so that they could no longer understand each other. The Lord did just that and the tower was left as it was and it was called, like the city, Babel.

THE PROMISE TO ABRAM

GENESIS 12

In one of these distant lands lived Abram and his wife, Sarai, and his brother's son, Lot. Abram was a good man and God had been watching him for many years. God spoke to Abram, making him this promise: that if Abram went where God would lead him, and settle there, God would make that land a great nation.

Abram did as God asked of him and with his family went into the land of Canaan. There he pitched his tent on a mountain, but it had not rained for a long time and the earth was dry and there was no food and Abram knew they would all die so he took his family to Egypt to stay until there was rain once more in Canaan.

Now Sarai was very beautiful and Abram was afraid the Egyptians would kill him if they knew Sarai was his wife so that they could marry her. So he told the Pharaoh who ruled the land that Sarai was his sister. Because all the princes *did* want to marry the beautiful Sarai they treated Abram very well and gave him sheep and oxen and many servants.

Then things began to go badly for the Pharaoh and Pharaoh blamed it on Abram and Sarai, but he let them both leave taking with them all that he had given them.

ABRAM AND LOT

GENESIS 13-15

When Abram returned to Canaan he was rich in cattle and silver and gold, but things were not the same and Abram quarrelled with Lot and there was trouble as well between the men who tended the cattle for Abram and the men who did the same thing for Lot.

"Let us not quarrel," Abram told Lot. "There is so much land." Abram held up his hands. "You take all the land on my left hand and I will take all the land on my right."

Lot could see that the land on the left was the plain of Jordan, and was green and had water and would be good for his cattle and so he thanked Abram and said "Goodbye" to his uncle and pitched his own tent near Sodom. But the people of Sodom and the twin city of Gomorrah were wicked people and there was a war in the land and Lot and all he owned were captured, but Abram rescued Lot and his goods and all his followers from the people of Sodom.

ABRAM BECOMES ABRAHAM

GENESIS 17

Abram was very unhappy because he and Sarai had no children and he was ninety-nine years old and Sarai was nearly as old. One day God spoke to him and said, "No longer will you be called Abram but Abraham, for you will be the father of many nations. I will give you the land of Canaan. Your wife, Sarai, shall now be called Sarah. I will bless her and she will have a son and become the mother of kings."

Abraham laughed. "But we are very old to have a son," he said.

"It shall happen," the Lord told him, "and because you could laugh at the Lord's word you will call your son Isaac which means '*he who will laugh.*'"

ABRAHAM AND THE LORD

GENESIS 18

In the city of Sodom where Lot remained the wickedness continued and the Lord spoke to Abraham about it. Abraham was frightened that the Lord would destroy the good people of Sodom with the wicked and Lot would be among them. The Lord told Abraham that if He found in Sodom fifty good people He would spare the entire city.

Abraham was very brave before the Lord and he spoke up. "If You find only forty-five good people would You destroy the city because there were not fifty?"

The Lord answered: "I shall spare the city if I find *forty* good people in Sodom."

Abraham grew braver. "And if there are only thirty good people?" he asked the Lord.

The Lord was angry but He told Abraham, "If I find ten good people Sodom will not be destroyed," and then He left Abraham standing there alone.

LOT'S WIFE

GENESIS 20

Lot sat at the gates of Sodom. Two Angels came to him and Lot rose and bowed. Then he invited the Angels to lodge at his house. Before nightfall the men of Sodom came to Lot's house and called to him, "Where are the men who came to you tonight?"

Lot went out to talk to the angry men. "Do not be so wicked," Lot told them. "I have two beautiful daughters and I shall give them to you but you must not touch these men."

"Stand back!" said the men and they nearly broke the door down but the Angels pulled Lot back into the house and then they went out and fought the men until they were gone.

"Take all your family out of this place," they told Lot, "for we are here to destroy it because it has become so evil and the people so wicked, but you are not."

The next morning the Angels and Lot and his family rose before sunrise and the Angels led Lot and his wife and his family to the gates of the city and told Lot, "Escape for your life, but *never look back.*"

By the time the sun had risen all of Sodom and nearby Gomorrah were burning but Lot and his family were all safe until Lot's wife looked back and lo! she became a bag of salt!

REBECCA AT THE WELL

As Abraham grew old he became worried that his son, Isaac, would not marry before he died. He asked his oldest and most trusted servant to do him one last great service.

"Go back to my country and among my people choose a wife for my son Isaac and bring her here."

"But what if the girl I choose won't come to Canaan with me?" the servant asked.

"If the girl will not come willingly then you shall come back alone, only do not take my son to that land."

The servant gave his hand to Abraham and he swore to do as his master had asked him.

The next morning the servant took ten of his master's camels and went to Mesopotamia. There he made the camels kneel down outside the city, beside a well at the time of the evening when the women and young girls went to draw the water.

The servant said to himself, "When I look up let there be a young girl to whom I shall say, 'Put down your pitcher that I may have a drink,' and she shall offer my camels a drink as well so I will know she is kind and a good wife for Abraham's son."

When the servant looked up there was a lovely girl named Rebecca with her water pitcher on her shoulder. The servant watched her as she went to the well and filled her pitcher. The servant ran to meet her.

"Please let me have a drink of water from your pitcher!" he cried.

"Drink, my lord," Rebecca said, and she gave him the pitcher to take as much water as he wished and then she said, "I will draw water for your camels as well," and she kept filling the trough for the camels to drink in until they had had enough.

THE SERVANT AT REBECCA'S HOUSE

GENESIS 24

The servant gave Rebecca a golden earring and two gold bracelets and she was very pleased.

"Whose daughter are you?" the servant asked.

"I am Rebecca, the daughter of Bethuel," she told him.

"Is there room in your father's house for us to stay for the night?" he asked.

"There is both straw to sleep on and room to lodge in," she replied.

And Rebecca's brother came to help lead the servant and the camels to their house. They set a fine dinner before him but he said to Rebecca's father, "I cannot eat until I tell you why I am here. I am Abraham's servant and I have come to Abraham's country to find a wife for his son, Isaac. I was not sure that a young girl would follow me willingly so today at the well I prayed and Rebecca appeared as if in answer to my prayers and led me here."

"It must surely be the wish of the Lord's," said Rebecca's father. "Take her to your master's son as a wife."

They called Rebecca and the servant asked her if she would come willingly with him.

"I will," said Rebecca, and then Rebecca and her handmaidens rode on the camels with the servant back to Canaan.

ISAAC AND REBECCA

GENESIS 24

Early one evening Isaac was sitting in his fields thinking of many things when he looked up and saw his father's servant coming towards him with ten camels. As the camels came closer Isaac saw Rebecca sitting on the front camel and Rebecca saw the handsome Isaac and knew immediately this was the man she was to marry. Isaac loved Rebecca from the very first moment and he took her back to his home and they were married.

27

THE TWINS—ESAU AND JACOB

GENESIS 25

Rebecca and Isaac lived very happily but it was many years before they had children. Then they had twins. The elder was called Esau and his younger brother, Jacob. Esau had thick red hair and grew to be a cunning hunter, but Jacob was a plain man who did not like to hunt. Isaac loved Esau more than Jacob because he liked the thought of his son being a hunter and this hurt Rebecca and she loved the younger brother all the more.

One day Jacob was cooking soup when Esau came from the field. He had been without food a long time and was hungry and faint. "Feed me," he begged his brother, "or I shall die of hunger."

"Sell me your birthright first," Jacob said, for Esau being the elder was to inherit all his father's wealth.

"I am so hungry I will do it," Esau said.

Esau swore to Jacob that he could have his birthright for a bowl of soup. *Then Jacob gave Esau the soup and bread* which had cost Esau his birthright.

THE DECEPTION

When Isaac was very old he became blind. He called Esau to him and said, "My son."

"Here I am," Esau assured him.

"I am old and I am dying. I want to bless you. Go get your bow and go out to the field and kill a deer. Then cook me the tasty meat which I love and I shall bless you."

Esau immediately did as his father told him. But Rebecca had overheard the conversation and she was worried that her younger son, Jacob, would not be blessed. So she spoke to Jacob.

"Obey me," she said, "go now to the flock and bring me two small kids and I will make a tasty meal for your father with them. He will then bless *you* and not your brother."

"But my father will feel me and know that I am Jacob because I haven't the full growth of hair that Esau has, and he will curse me instead of blessing me because I have lied to him."

"Obey me," his mother said. "It will be my curse then, not yours."

Jacob got the two small kids and his mother made a tasty meal of them. Then she took Esau's robes and put them on Jacob and put the skins of the kids around his neck so his hair would seem longer to the touch and she gave Jacob the food and he went with it to his father.

"My father," he said.

"Which son are you?" Isaac asked.

"I am Esau. I have done as you asked me."

"Come near that I may feel you," Isaac said.

Jacob went near him and Isaac felt him. "The voice sounds like Jacob's voice but surely it does feel like Esau. Bring the food near me and I shall eat."

Jacob brought the food to his father and Isaac ate and afterwards he said, "Come near now and kiss me, my son."

Jacob came very close and Isaac kissed him and as he did he smelled his robes and he said: "It is Esau, for your robes smell of the fields. I will bless you. God will give you rich lands and good crops and people will serve you and nations bow down to you. You will be lord over your brother and anyone who curses you shall be cursed themselves."

As soon as Isaac had given his blessing and Jacob had left, Esau returned from his hunting. He also made a tasty meal for his father and brought it to him.

"Who are you?" his father asked.

"I am Esau, father."

Isaac trembled. "Where is your brother who said he was you and whom I have already blessed as you?"

Esau cried bitterly when he heard these words. "Bless me too, father!"

Isaac said, "I cannot go against my word. I have made him your lord and given him servants and your fields."

Esau hated Jacob and vowed he would kill him after his father's death! Rebecca heard of Esau's vow and she called Jacob to her and told him to go to his uncle Laban's home in Haran and stay there until Esau's anger was gone.

31

JACOB LEAVES

Rebecca told Isaac that she was unhappy because Jacob had not married a girl from their own country of Haran, and so Isaac called Jacob to him and told him to travel to his mother's house and marry one of his fair cousins. And he blessed Jacob again and sent him away. And so Jacob was free of Esau's anger.

JACOB'S DREAM

Jacob set out on his journey and travelled until the sun had set. Then he took a stone for his pillow and lay down to sleep. He dreamed there was a ladder set up on earth and the top of it reached into Heaven and there were Angels of God going up and down it and the Lord Himself stood at the very top and said in His God's voice, "I am *the Lord*. The land where you sleep I give to you. I am with you and will keep you safe."

Jacob woke and he was very frightened. He looked around him and thought *what a dreadful place this is*. He took the stone he had used for a pillow and let it mark the place and he called the place Beth-el.

Jacob said, "If God will be with me so that I can come again in peace to my father's house, then shall the Lord be my God, and the stone which marks this place shall mark a House of God."

33

RACHEL

GENESIS 29

Jacob continued his journey and finally came to a new land. He saw a well in a field and three flocks of sheep lying by it.

"My brothers, where are you from?" Jacob asked the shepherds.

"We are from Haran," they said.

"Do you know my uncle, Laban?" he asked them. They said, "We know him."

"Is he well?" Jacob asked.

"Yes," they replied, "but ask his daughter, Rachel, yourself because she is coming with the sheep."

Rachel ran to tell her father about her cousin's arrival and Laban returned with her. When he saw Jacob he embraced him and brought him back to his house and asked Jacob to remain with him, and work for him until his brother's anger was gone.

"But I must pay you," Laban said. "How much shall that be?"

Now Laban had two daughters and Rachel was the younger. She had an older sister named Leah. Leah was gentle and good but not as beautiful as Rachel. Jacob had loved Rachel from the moment he saw her and so he said, "I will serve you seven years for your daughter Rachel's hand in marriage."

Jacob did serve seven years for Rachel and they seemed to him but a few days because he loved Rachel dearly.

THE WEDDING

At the end of the seven years Jacob came to Laban and said, "I have served you well for seven years. Now my time is up. Give me my wife so that I may leave."

Laban made a great wedding feast, but that evening in the darkness Laban brought Leah to Jacob and Jacob, thinking she was Rachel, married her. When Jacob found he had married Leah he went to Laban.

"What have you done?" he said. "Didn't I serve you for Rachel? Why have you done this to me?"

"In our country it must be this way, because the youngest cannot marry before the first-born and no one has asked for Leah's hand all these seven years. But if you will promise to serve me another seven years I will give you Rachel for a wife, too."

So Jacob took Rachel as his wife also for it was the custom in that time for a man to have more than one wife; Jacob loved Rachel more than Leah but Leah gave Jacob many sons. Then Rachel had a son and she called her son Joseph.

JACOB STEALS AWAY FROM HARAN

It was now twenty years since Jacob had come to claim Rachel for his wife and he was very rich. Rachel's brothers were jealous of him and one day Jacob heard them saying, "Jacob has taken away all the wealth that would be ours."

Jacob called Leah and Rachel to him. "God has spoken to me and told me to return to the land of my father, but you are my wives. I must ask you first if we should leave the land of your father," he said.

"Our father looks at us as strangers," said Rachel.

"He sold us and used our money and left us without inheritance," Leah said.

"Whatever God has told you to do, do and we will go with you," they both said.

So Jacob put all his children and his wives on camels and took with him all his cattle and his belongings and stole away when Laban was in the fields. He fled from Haran over the river towards the mountains.

JACOB IS FOLLOWED

Laban was in the fields for three days and when he came back and found that Jacob had fled he was very angry. He took his brothers and followed Jacob until a week later he overtook him on Mount Gilead.

But God spoke to Laban and warned him not to harm Jacob.

Jacob had pitched his tent on the mountain-side and Laban and his brothers pitched their tents close by.

Then Laban spoke to Jacob: "Why did you steal away without telling me, taking my daughters and my grandchildren with you? I could strike you but the Lord God spoke to me and I can do you no harm, yet why have you stolen my goods?"

"I have stolen nothing of yours. Search my followers and my camels and if you find anything of yours then kill that person who stole it!" Jacob said.

But Jacob did not know that Rachel *had* stolen some statues of her father's and hid them under her camel's saddle and was sitting on them! When Laban came close to her she said, "I am sorry, my lord, but I cannot rise for I am ill."

Jacob grew angry because Laban wanted to search his own daughters! "You have searched my belongings," he said, "and found nothing! For fourteen years I served you for your two daughters and six more years for your cattle. You have changed my wages ten times and had you not heard God's word you would have sent me away empty-handed. God saw my suffering and He told you not to harm me, otherwise you would have killed me and taken back my wives and my cattle."

Laban said, "I could do you no harm. I swear it!"

Jacob then took a stone and set it in the ground and told his men to gather more stones and they made a great pile of stones and Laban said, "I will not pass over this pile of stones to harm you and you shall not pass over them to harm me."

Then they ate on the stone pile and in the morning Laban rose and kissed his sons and daughters and blessed them and returned to his own land.

JACOB'S GIFTS TO ESAU

Jacob went on his way but before he had gone far he sent messengers on ahead to tell Esau that he came in peace and that he had stayed with their uncle Laban all these years. The messengers came back telling Jacob his brother was coming to meet him with four hundred men.

Jacob was greatly afraid! He divided all his people in two groups, so that if Esau attacked one group the other would be able to escape. Then he made a present of two hundred goats and two hundred lambs and thirty camels and ten bulls and twenty donkeys and he told his servants to take the present to Esau. Then Jacob sat alone all night waiting for Esau to come.

THE MEETING OF JACOB AND ESAU

GENESIS 33

The next morning Esau came and with him four hundred men. Jacob divided the children between Leah, Rachel and the two handmaids. He put the handmaids and their children in the front and Leah and her children next and Rachel and Joseph last He went ahead of them and bowed to the ground seven times until he was near his brother. Esau ran to meet him and embraced him and then he saw the women and the children.

"Who are they?" Esau asked.

"My children," Jacob said. They were no longer afraid and the women and children all came close and bowed as Jacob had.

"You did not have to send presents, my brother. I have enough. Keep what is yours for yourself," Esau said.

"No," Jacob told him. "Keep my gifts and take my blessing."

And the two brothers smiled upon each other and Esau took his brother's gifts.

"Let us start our journey," Esau said. "I will go before you."

"It is a harder journey for women and children, my brother, and we cannot go fast," Jacob said.

"Then I will leave some of my men and make your way safe."

"Why," asked Jacob, "when there is peace now between us?"

So Esau left and Jacob and his followers went on until they came to the city of Shalem and there he pitched his tent and bought a parcel of land for one hundred pieces of money and he put up an altar on the land and called it El-elohe—Israel.

JOSEPH AND HIS BROTHERS

GENESIS 37

Rachel gave birth to another son whom she and Jacob named Benjamin. Then Rachel died. Joseph grew to be a handsome boy, who loved his baby brother, Benjamin. Every day he would go to the fields with his brothers and feed the sheep. Jacob loved Joseph more than all his sons and he made him a coat of many colours. When his brothers saw the beautiful coat they became jealous.

One day, while feeding the flock, Joseph told his brothers, "I had a dream and in this dream I was tying together a bundle of corn and it stood straight up! And you were all doing the same thing and your bundles of corn also stood up—but they bowed to me."

His brothers became even more jealous because Joseph dreamed they would bow to him as if he were their king, and they sent him away from them. Joseph went to his father who told him to go after his brothers. Joseph did but he could not find them and became lost. An old man found him wandering alone in the fields.

"What are you looking for?" the old man asked.

"My brothers."

"Oh, they have left and gone to Dotham."

So Joseph went after his brothers and found them in Dotham. When they saw Joseph their first thoughts were to kill him.

One of his brothers said, "We can kill him and throw him into a pit and say a wild animal ate him up and then we shall see what happens to his beautiful dreams!"

But his brother, Reuben, was a gentler sort. "Let us not kill him," he said. "Throw him into a pit if you must but do not harm him." He said this because he was planning to save Joseph and bring him home to his father again.

Joseph was taken captive by his brothers and they took away his coat of many colours and threw him into a pit that had no water and then they settled down to eat their evening meal, but as they did so a band of Ishmaelites came along with their camels loaded with spices they were taking to Egypt.

One of the brothers then had an idea. Why not sell Joseph to the Ishmaelites and make some money as well as rid themselves of him? They all agreed and they lifted the young Joseph out of the pit and sold him for twenty pieces of silver, but the kindly brother Reuben had gone off to get some food for Joseph and when he returned Joseph was gone!

Then the brothers took the coat of many colours and killed a small animal and dipped the coat into the animal's blood and brought the coat back to Jacob, who mourned for his son so much that no one, not even the baby, Benjamin, could console him.

And Joseph in the meantime had been taken into Egypt and sold to Pharaoh's captain of the guard.

JOSEPH IN EGYPT

GENESIS 39

Joseph did well with his master, Potiphar, the captain of the Pharaoh's guards, in Egypt. Potiphar made him overseer of his estáte and put everything in his hands. Joseph was good and the Lord was with him, and Potiphar could see that.

One day Joseph, who had grown to be a handsome young man, was left alone in the house with his master's wife, who had fallen in love with him. She begged Joseph to love her, too. Joseph told her he could never love her because it would be a sin and because his master trusted him.

Potiphar's wife was furious! She went to Potiphar and lied to him and told him Joseph had said terrible things to her and Potiphar could do nothing else but send Joseph to prison.

But the Lord was with Joseph and showed him mercy, and the keeper of the prison liked Joseph and was good to him and let him be in charge of many other prisoners, and Joseph was good to them.

THE BUTLER AND THE BAKER

GENESIS 40

While Joseph was in prison both the Pharaoh's chief butler and the Pharaoh's chief baker were sent there for displeasing the Pharaoh and they were placed in Joseph's care.

Both of them dreamed a dream in the same night and when Joseph came to them in the morning they looked very sad.

"Why do you look so sad today?" Joseph asked.

"We each dreamed a dream and do not know what the dream means," they told him.

"Tell me the dreams," he said.

So the chief butler told his dream to Joseph. "In my dream there was a vine and in the vine were three branches and there were blossoms and clusters of grapes, and the Pharaoh's cup was in my hand; I took the grapes and pressed them into the Pharaoh's cup and gave it to the Pharaoh."

"Ah, well," said Joseph. "The three branches were three days. In three days the Pharaoh will make you once again the chief butler, so I ask you to remember my kindness to you and mention it to the Pharaoh so that I may be released from here."

Then the chief baker, pleased with what Joseph had said about the chief butler's dream, told him his own. "I also was in my dreams and I had three white baskets on my head and in the top basket were the Pharaoh's sweets and the birds ate all of them up so that I had none when I reached the Pharaoh."

Joseph looked sadly at the chief baker. "Your three baskets are three days as well, but in three days the Pharaoh will hang you from a tree and there will be birds on the branches."

In three days the chief butler was released and the baker was hanged as Joseph had said.

Still, the chief butler did not tell the Pharaoh of Joseph's kindness to him.

THE PHARAOH'S DREAM

GENESIS 41

Two full years passed and Joseph was still in prison. But the Pharaoh now had a dream that he stood by the river and seven fat cows came out of the water to feed in the nearby meadow and then seven scrawny cows came out of the water and they went to the nearby meadow and they ate up the seven fat cows. The dream woke the Pharaoh. Finally he fell back to sleep again but he dreamed another dream! This time seven ears of corn came up as one stalk. They were strong and sweet and then seven more ears of corn came up but they were shrivelled and frail and the seven shrivelled ears of corn ate up the seven strong and sweet ears of corn.

The Pharaoh woke up again and this time he could not go back to sleep because he was very disturbed. He sent for all the magicians in Egypt but they could

not tell him what the dream meant. Then he sent for all the wise men of the land, but they were unable to tell him what his dream meant, either. The Pharaoh was very unhappy; then the chief butler remembered Joseph.

"Once," he told the Pharaoh, "when you were angry with me you put me in prison with the chief baker. One night we each had a dream and there was with us a young man, a Hebrew, who was a servant to the captain of the guards and we told him our dreams and he told us what they meant and it happened just as he said!"

The Pharaoh sent for Joseph. "I have had two dreams," he told Joseph, "and my magicians and my wise men cannot tell me what they mean but my chief butler tells me you could tell me the meaning."

"If there is a meaning God will give it to the Pharaoh," Joseph said.

And so Pharaoh told Joseph his two dreams and Joseph listened very attentively. When the Pharaoh was finished he said, "The two dreams are really one. God has shown Pharaoh what He is about to do. The seven good cows and the seven good ears of corn are seven years. The dream is the same. The seven scrawny cows that came after are also seven years and the seven shrivelled ears of corn will be seven years of hunger in your land. God is showing Pharaoh that you will have seven years of plenty throughout the whole land of Egypt and then seven years of hunger when all the plenty shall be forgotten. The dream was sent to Pharaoh twice because it will happen soon. Therefore, Pharaoh must find a wise man to look over the crops and appoint officers who will take a fifth of the fat crop during the seven years of plenty so that there will be food for the seven years of hunger."

The Pharaoh said, "Your plan is wise, Joseph, and you are a wise man. I will place you in charge of the land and see that this is done."

And the Pharaoh took the ring from his hand and put it on Joseph's hand and he gave him fine linen robes to wear and a golden chain for around his neck and bade him ride in his second finest chariot, and the people bowed before him as Pharaoh made him ruler over all the land of Egypt and only second in power to the Pharaoh himself.

Then he gave Joseph the beautiful Asenath, who was the daughter of the Priest of On, to be his wife.

THE SEVEN YEARS OF PLENTY PASS

GENESIS 41

There were, as Joseph said there would be, seven years of plenty and he gathered up all the food he could store and kept it in the cities and near the fields. There was so much food that there was almost no place left to store it.

Joseph's wife, the beautiful Asenath, gave birth to two sons. They called the elder Manasseh and the younger Ephraim.

Then the seven years of plenty ended and the seven years of hunger began. The people cried to Pharaoh for bread and Pharaoh told them, "Go to Joseph and do as he says."

Joseph opened the storehouses and gave the Egyptians food. There was enough to send to other lands because the hunger had spread, and people from other countries came to Egypt to pay homage to Joseph and buy the food he had stored.

JOSEPH'S BROTHERS GO TO EGYPT

GENESIS 42

The hunger reached the land of Canaan where Joseph's father, Jacob, and Joseph's brothers still lived. Jacob heard there was corn and food in Egypt, so he told his ten sons, keeping Benjamin by his side, to go to Egypt and buy food for all of them, and they set off as their father asked.

Joseph was now lord of the land and very powerful and anyone who wanted food had to come to him first. It had been so many years since the brothers had seen Joseph that they no longer knew who he was, but when they came before him and bowed down to him Joseph recognised them.

"Where are you from?" he asked.

"The land of Canaan," they said, still on their knees.

"You are spies!" he told them.

"Oh, no, my lord! We have come only to buy food!"

"I do not believe you."

"But it is so, my lord. We are twelve brothers, the sons of Jacob in the land of Canaan. Our youngest brother is with our father and another brother is dead."

"I still do not believe you, but I will give you the chance to prove that what you say is true. All except one of you will be held in prison and that one will travel to Canaan and bring back with him your youngest brother."

But the brothers could not agree on which one should go because they did not trust each other. So Joseph placed them under guard for three days and at the end of that time he came to them.

"If you do not trust each other, how can I trust you?" he said. Then he took his brother, Simeon,

and tied him up before their eyes. Then he told them, "Go. I will keep this brother here until you bring me back your youngest brother."

Joseph told his men to fill his brothers' sacks with corn and he placed the money they gave him back into the sacks without their knowing it. Then they loaded their donkeys and left Simeon and Egypt.

THE BROTHERS RETURN TO CANAAN
GENESIS 42

When the brothers reached Canaan they opened their sacks and found the money. They were very frightened of what the lord of Egypt might do if he thought they had not paid for their food. Then they went to Jacob and told him, "There is a man who is lord over all of Egypt and he took us for spies. We told him we were only twelve brothers, the sons of Jacob, and that Benjamin, still being a child, was with you and that another brother was dead. But he still did not believe us and he tied Simeon up before our eyes and sent us on our way with corn and food in all our sacks, but he told us we must bring Benjamin back to him so that he would know we had not lied. Only then would he release Simeon."

"And when we emptied our sacks," another brother added, "we found the same money we had paid for the corn and now we are very frightened."

"How could this happen?" Jacob cried. "First I lose Rachel's son, Joseph. Now Simeon is a prisoner and you ask me to give up Rachel's only other son, Benjamin. I cannot do it. This man may kill you all!"

54

Reuben beseeched his father, "I saw a kindness in this man's eyes. When he sees Benjamin he will know we tell the truth and return Simeon to our side."

"No!" Jacob said. "I shall not let you take Benjamin. Joseph, his only true brother, is dead and he is all that is left to me of Rachel."

And Jacob would talk of it no more, though he was saddened that Simeon was a prisoner in a foreign land.

JACOB SENDS BENJAMIN

GENESIS 43

But soon all the food the brothers had brought back from Egypt was gone and their wives and children and servants were starving and they went to speak to Jacob again.

"Go to Egypt and buy food," he told them finally.

"But this man said we could not return without Benjamin. If you will send Benjamin with us we will go, otherwise he may kill us all!"

But Jacob still did not want Benjamin to leave Canaan.

"If you do not let him go, all of us will die of hunger; your sons and their wives and your grandchildren."

It was very difficult for Jacob but he knew his sons were right, so he said, "Bring this man a present and double the money so that he will know you intended to pay last time and it was a mistake that the money was returned in your sacks." Then he looked at Benjamin and held him close. "May God Almighty see all of you return safely." Then he kissed Benjamin and Benjamin went with his brothers to Egypt.

BENJAMIN AND JOSEPH

The brothers arrived in Egypt and went at once to see Joseph. When Joseph saw Benjamin he had the brothers brought to his house. The brothers were afraid because they thought Joseph would take them as slaves and keep their donkeys, and all because of the money that had been found the previous time in their sacks!

As they neared Joseph's house they said to Joseph's manservant, "Oh, sir, the first time we only came to buy food and when we arrived in Canaan and opened our sacks all our money had been returned. We have brought it back to your lord again with more money for more food. We do not know who put that money in our sacks!"

"Fear not," the servant told them. "Your God gave you the money you found. I received your money."

Then he brought Simeon out to them and Simeon was well and so they went with the servant into Joseph's house and the man told them that they were to eat there. When Joseph came home they all bowed to him again and gave him their presents.

"How are you?" he asked. "And is the old man, your father, alive?"

"We are well but hungry and our father is still alive and in good health," and they bowed again to Joseph.

Then Joseph saw Benjamin and he said softly, "Is that your youngest brother?"

"Yes, my lord."

Joseph came close to Benjamin. "God be with you, child," he said, gently. Benjamin looked up at Joseph and it struck Joseph how much like their mother the child looked and he felt near to tears because it had been a long time since he had been with his small brother. And he left them and went to his own room and wept with happiness. Then he washed his face and returned to his brothers and told his servants, "Serve the food!" And when the food was served Benjamin had five times that of his other brothers.

THE SILVER DRINKING CUP

When they had done eating Joseph ordered his servants to fill his brothers' sacks with as much food as
they could carry and to return their money again to

them in the sacks. "And," he went on, "Put my silver cup in the sack of the youngest along with his money."

The servant did everything Joseph had ordered.

As soon as the morning was light the brothers were sent away and when they were out of the city Joseph told his servant, "Follow them and when you overtake them, say, 'You have done evil. One of you has stolen my lord's silver drinking cup'."

The man soon caught up with the brothers. "You have done evil," he said to them. "One of you has stolen my lord's silver drinking cup!"

"How could your lord say such a thing? Didn't we bring back the money we found in our sacks from the last trip? Why should we steal silver or gold from your lord's house?"

"If this is so," another brother said, "whoever is found to have this drinking cup will die at your hands and the rest of us will be your lord's slaves!"

But Joseph had told his servant otherwise. "No," the servant said, "my lord only wants the thief; the rest of you shall be able to go on your way."

Then each man quickly put his sack on the ground and opened it. The sacks were all searched, starting with the oldest brother until, at last, Benjamin's sack was searched and, of course, the silver drinking-cup was there!

The brothers could not believe it! They went back to Joseph's house and fell down on the ground before him.

"How can we clear ourselves?" his brother, Judah, asked. "We shall *all* be your slaves as well as the one in whose sack you found the silver cup."

"No," said Joseph, "only he shall remain. The rest of you go in peace to your father."

JUDAH PLEADS FOR BENJAMIN

Joseph's half-brother, Judah, came closer to Joseph to beseech him, "Oh, my lord," he cried, "please don't take your anger out on the boy! Our father is

an old man and the boy was born when he was already old and the boy's mother and his only true brother are both dead and our father loves him dearly! You asked us to bring the boy to you and we told you the lad could not leave his father for if he did his father would die! Had we not all been starving we would not be here. But our father said to us before we took this second journey, 'My wife, Rachel, had two sons. One is dead. If anything should happen to Benjamin I would die, too', and if we return without the lad he will surely die! I beg you! Take me in the lad's place as your slave so that my father shall live!"

Joseph was moved by Judah. He told all his servants to leave the room and then he stood facing his brothers.

"I am your brother Joseph!" he cried, and his brothers were frightened. "Come closer," he told them. Still frightened, they came closer. "I am truly your brother Joseph whom you sold as a slave, but do not be sad or angry for God sent me here through you so that I could save your lives. There has been famine in the land for two years but there are still five years in which the corn will not grow. Go now to our father and tell him that his son, Joseph, is lord over all Egypt and ask him to join me here with all of you and your wives and your children and I will keep you well fed during the time of hunger!"

"It cannot be Joseph!" his brothers said.

Joseph held Benjamin to him. "See how much we look alike," he said.

And even though Joseph wore fine robes and gold rings, his brothers could see what he said was the truth. Benjamin held on to Joseph's robes and hugged him, and Joseph and his brothers talked and the past was soon forgotten.

JACOB GOES TO EGYPT

Joseph told the Pharaoh about his brothers and his father and the Pharaoh told him to have all his family, even his brothers' wives and children, come to Egypt. When Jacob heard Joseph was alive he started out to see his son, taking all his family with him. And Joseph, in his beautiful chariot, went to meet his father.

It was a very happy meeting and Joseph told his father to tell the Pharaoh that they were shepherds and his father agreed and then Jacob rode in Joseph's chariot to see the Pharaoh.

JACOB MEETS THE PHARAOH

GENESIS 47

Joseph brought Jacob before the Pharaoh.

"How old are you?" the Pharaoh asked.

"One hundred and thirty," Jacob told him. Then he blessed the Pharaoh and the Pharaoh gave Jacob and his family the land of Rameses to tend their sheep and cattle, and Joseph made sure his family all had enough food to eat during all the years of the famine.

JACOB'S PROPHECY

GENESIS 49-50

The hunger passed and soon the land was rich again and filled with grain. Jacob was now very old indeed and he knew the time had come when he would die, so he called his twelve sons together.

"I will tell you now," he said when they were all together, "what will become of you. From you twelve, the twelve tribes of Israel shall be born. Judah's tribe will be the one that will be the greatest but all of you will be blessed."

Then Jacob lay back on his bed and closed his eyes for ever and Joseph and all Egypt mourned his father for seventy days. Then he placed his father's fine coffin on his chariot and went back to Canaan. But Joseph returned again to Egypt and he forgave his brothers for the evil thing they had done when he was a boy.

EXODUS

THE BIRTH OF MOSES

Before Jacob, Joseph's father, died God gave him the name of Israel. Therefore, all his children and his grandchildren and all the children after them were called the children of Israel.

It was many years since Joseph and his sons had lived and there was a new Pharaoh in Egypt who did

not know the wonderful things Joseph had done. The children of Israel were strong and wise and the new Pharaoh feared they would rise and fight against the Egyptians and overcome them. He therefore made them slaves and made them build great cities for him and worked them very hard. But the harder the Pharaoh made them work the stronger the children of Israel became.

The Pharaoh became angrier still and he spoke to the people and said, "If a Hebrew child [for so also were called the children of Israel] is born, if it is a son, the nurse shall kill it; but if it is a daughter it may live."

But the nurses would not kill the baby boys. The Pharaoh grew angrier yet and he spoke to the nurses, "Why have you not done as I commanded?"

"Oh, Pharaoh," the nurses replied, "the Hebrew women are not like the Egyptian women. They have no need for nurses when they have their children, and so how can we tell if a Hebrew child, son or daughter, has been born at all?"

The Pharaoh then spoke to the children of Israel himself. "Every son you have," he told them, "must be thrown into the river! Only your daughters may live."

But one of the children of Israel had a son and he was so good and beautiful that his mother could not do as the Pharaoh commanded. She took a small basket made of bullrushes and put the baby into it and brought it down to the river's bank and hid it safely in the tall green grass that grew by the sides of the river.

PHARAOH'S DAUGHTER FINDS MOSES

EXODUS 2

Very soon after, the Pharaoh's daughter came down to the river with her handmaidens to wash herself and when she saw the basket in the tall grass she sent them to bring it to her.

The Pharaoh's daughter picked up the baby and saw how beautiful it was. She was very sad because she knew it was a Hebrew child and a boy. But the baby's sister had been watching her brother in the basket all the time and drew close to the Pharaoh's daughter.

"Shall I find a nurse from the Hebrew women?" she asked the princess.

"Yes," said the princess, still holding the beautiful child.

The little girl ran to get her mother and when they returned the princess said to her, "Take this baby and nurse it for me and I shall pay you for it."

So the mother took her own child from the princess and took care of him. And when he was old enough she brought him back to the princess who named him Moses because that meant "saved," and she had saved Moses from being drowned.

MOSES AT THE WELL

EXODUS 2

When Moses had grown into a young man he came upon an Egyptian striking a Hebrew. Moses looked behind him and thought he was quite alone so he killed the Egyptian and then hid him in the sand. The next day he went walking again and this time he saw a Hebrew striking another Hebrew!

"Why are you hitting your own brother?" Moses asked the guilty one.

"Why should you ask that when you have killed an Egyptian?" the man asked Moses.

Moses knew then that what he had done had been seen and that soon the Pharaoh would find out as well, and so he ran away and kept on going until he reached the land of Midian and here by a well he finally rested.

Now the priest of Midian had seven daughters and they came to draw water from the well. As they did, some neighbouring shepherds frightened them and would not let them do so. Moses stood up and the shepherds, fearing Moses, left. Moses helped the women water their father's sheep. When they returned to their father he asked, "How is it you have finished your work so quickly today?"

"There was an Egyptian who helped us water the flock," they told him.

"Where is this man and why did you not invite him to share our food?" the father asked, and sent them to get Moses.

Moses came to live with the priest and his daughters and fell in love with the one called Zipporah. They had a son and Moses called him Gershon which means "a stranger there," because Moses had been a stranger in this land.

GOD SPEAKS TO MOSES

EXODUS 3-4

Moses was tending the sheep for his father-in-law, the priest of Midian. One day while he led the flock a nearby bush caught fire and there were great flames but when the fire was out the bush was not burnt. Moses went closer to see why the bush had not burnt.

"Moses, Moses!" It was the voice of God.

"Here I am," Moses replied.

"Do not come any closer until you take off your shoes, for the ground on which you are standing is holy ground."

Moses took off his shoes and came closer to the bush.

"I have seen how your people have suffered," God told him. "I have heard them cry and I am going to bring them out of Egypt into a beautiful land of milk and honey. You are to go to the Pharaoh and lead my people, the children of Israel, out of Egypt."

But Moses asked the Lord, "How can I?"

"I will be with you," God told him, "and when you have done as I say you shall say your prayers to *Me* upon this mountain."

"When I tell the children of Israel 'the God of your fathers has sent me,' they will ask your name. What shall I say to them?"

"'The Lord God of your Fathers, the God of Abraham, the God of Isaac and the God of Jacob has sent me. His name is Jehovah, and He appeared before me and told me how the children of Israel have suffered in Egypt and told me to lead you into another land'. They will listen to you. Then you shall go with the older men to the Pharaoh and tell him, 'The Lord God of the Hebrews has called us and we beg you to grant us three days to travel to His mountain in the wilderness and say prayers to Him.' I am sure the Pharaoh will not let you go but I will perform wonders and after that he will let you go, and when he does you shall not go empty-handed."

"They won't believe me," Moses said. "They shall say, 'The Lord has not appeared to you'."

"What is it that you have in your hand?" the Lord asked.

"A rod."

"Throw it on the ground."

Moses did and the rod became a snake! "Now take the serpent by the tail," the Lord commanded. Moses did and the snake became a rod again! "Now," the Lord continued, "put your hand against your chest." Moses did this and when he took it away it was white as snow and not like his hand at all. "Now put your hand against your chest again." Moses did and this time when he took it away it was once more his own hand.

"If they do not believe you or listen to you by the first sign, then they should believe the second sign, but if they do not, then you shall take water from the river and pour it on the dry land and it will become blood."

But Moses was still not sure. "O my Lord. I am not a good speaker," he apologised.

"Who has made man's mouth? Was it not I? Go. I will be your voice."

"I beg You send someone else," Moses said.

God became angry with Moses and would listen no longer. "Your brother, Aaron, speaks well and he will come to meet you. I will show both of you what to do. Now! Take the rod in your hand and go!"

MOSES GOES BACK TO EGYPT

Moses went home and asked his father-in-law to let him return to Egypt to see if his own family might still be alive.

"Go in peace," his father-in-law said.

Then God, pleased with Moses, told him he could return to Egypt without fear, as all the men who knew about the Egyptian he had killed were now dead. Then God spoke to Moses' brother, Aaron. "Go into the wilderness to meet Moses," He said. Aaron went and he and Moses met at the Mountain of God. Moses told Aaron all that the Lord had told him and all the signs He asked him to make.

Moses and Aaron then went back to Egypt and gathered together all the fathers of the Hebrews and Aaron spoke all the words to them that God had spoken to Moses and he did all the signs for the people to see.

The people believed Aaron and Moses and, when they heard that the Lord had seen their suffering and had sent Moses to lead them out of Egypt, they bowed their heads and gave thanks.

THE CRUEL PHARAOH

EXODUS 5

Moses and Aaron went into the Pharaoh's palace. "The Lord God has spoken to us," they said. "He has said that you must let our people go so that they may hold a feast in His honour in the wilderness."

"Who is the Lord, that I, Pharaoh of all Egypt, should obey His voice? I will not do as He says," the Pharaoh said, angrily.

"Let us go, we beg you, or else our Lord will be angry and cause us death and sickness."

But the Pharaoh made the Hebrews work even harder. "You shall no longer give the people straw to make the bricks as you have so kindly done in the past," he told his officers. "Let them gather straw for themselves. But they shall have to make the same number of bricks. The men will have no time then to listen to empty talk of a God."

The Pharaoh's officers did as the Pharaoh said and they stood over the children of Israel with whips, as if they were animals. The children of Israel then went to the Pharaoh.

"Why do you beat us when we are working as hard as we can?" they cried.

"Go from my presence!" the Pharaoh replied. "You will not be idle a minute to think of your God!"

The Hebrews left the Pharaoh's presence and they met Moses and Aaron. "You have made the Pharaoh hate us even more!" they shouted. "Next he will kill us all!"

GOD RENEWS HIS PROMISE

EXODUS 6

Moses spoke to the Lord again. "Since I spoke to the Pharaoh as You told me to do," Moses said, "the Pharaoh has been even crueller to the children of Israel and You have let this happen!"

Then the Lord said to Moses: "Now you shall see what I will do to the Pharaoh so that he will make our people leave Egypt. You speak to the children of Israel and tell them the Lord God will free them from slavery and make them His people and will lead them to the Promised Land."

Moses repeated the Lord's words to the children of Israel, but they would not listen.

God spoke to Moses again: "Go to the Pharaoh again and let Aaron tell him to let the children of Israel leave his land."

"If my own people will not listen to me, why should the Pharaoh?" Moses asked the Lord.

The Lord God replied, "You will do as I say. Aaron shall speak to the Pharaoh and tell him to send the children of Israel out of his land. If the Pharaoh does not do as I command, then I shall send My own armies into Egypt and his people shall suffer, but the children of Israel will remain safe to leave his land."

THE MAGIC RODS

Moses and Aaron went to the Pharaoh and said what the Lord had commanded. Then Aaron threw down his rod and it became a snake!

The Pharaoh called his wise men and his magicians. They all threw down their rods and all the rods became snakes; but Aaron's rod, which was the largest snake, consumed the others until there were none but Aaron's.

But the Pharaoh still would not do as the Lord God of the Hebrews demanded.

THE TEN PLAGUES

ONE: THE PLAGUE UPON THE RIVER

EXODUS 7

Then the Lord spoke to Moses: "Tell Aaron," He said, "to take your rod and wave it over the waters of Egypt, over their streams and their ponds, and even their pools of water, and the water will become blood."

Moses and Aaron did as the Lord God commanded with Pharaoh and all his servants watching and all the water *did* become blood! The fish that were in the rivers died and the Egyptians could not drink the water. The Pharaoh's wise men and magicians could do nothing to stop this terrible plague but the Pharaoh went back to his palace and still refused to let the children of Israel go.

The Egyptians dug around the river to find water to drink but for seven days there was none.

TWO: THE PLAGUE OF THE FROGS

EXODUS 8

After the seven days the Lord spoke again to Moses. "Go to Pharaoh," He told Moses, "and say to him, 'Let my people go, for if you do not, the Lord God will send a plague of frogs which shall go into your houses and your bedrooms and on to your beds, and into the houses of all the people of Egypt and even into their ovens.' Tell Aaron to wave your rod over the streams and it shall happen as I say."

Moses went to the Pharaoh and he still refused to let the children of Israel leave Egypt. Aaron then took the rod and waved it over all the rivers and the frogs came up and on to the land. Pharaoh called Moses to him. "Entreat your Lord to take away the frogs and I will let your people go," he said.

"When shall I do this?" Moses asked.

"Tomorrow," the Pharaoh replied.

"It shall be done as you say so that you will see that there is no one like the Lord our God. The frogs will disappear from the land and return to the rivers."

Moses prayed to the Lord and the Lord made the frogs disappear, but when the Pharaoh saw the frogs were gone he changed his mind and still refused to let the children of Israel go.

THREE: THE PLAGUE OF THE LICE

Then the Lord told Moses: "Tell Aaron to take your rod and strike the earth with it and then the dust will become lice and the lice will spread all over Egypt."

Aaron did this and it was as the Lord said.

The magicians could not make the lice disappear and they said to the Pharaoh, "This is the finger of God," but the Pharaoh still refused to let the children of Israel go.

FOUR: THE PLAGUE OF THE FLIES

EXODUS 8

The Lord then told Moses to rise early in the morning and meet the Pharaoh when he would be standing by the river. "Tell him," God said, "that I will send swarms of flies over all Egyptian homes but in the homes of the children of Israel there shall be no flies so he shall know *I am the Lord.*"

And the Lord did as He said He would.

Pharaoh called Moses to him. "I will let you go so that you can pray to your Lord in the wilderness, but you shall not go too far away."

"I will ask the Lord to make the flies disappear but, Pharaoh, you must not lie to us again and not let our people go."

Moses left the Pharaoh and prayed to the Lord and the Lord made all the flies disappear. But the Pharaoh went back on his word and still did not let the children of Israel go.

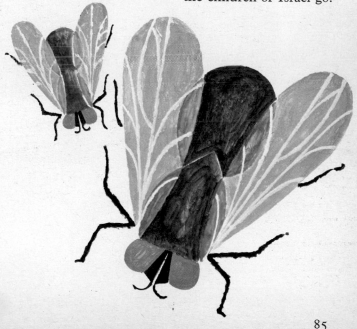

FIVE: THE PLAGUE OF THE CATTLE

EXODUS 9

Moses went to the Pharaoh again. "My Lord says you shall let His people go. He will give you until tomorrow and if you still refuse there shall be another terrible plague and all your horses and donkeys and camels and sheep and oxen and cattle shall die, but nothing that belongs to the children of Israel shall die."

The Pharaoh still would not do as Moses asked and so the next day all the cattle and horses and oxen and sheep and camels of the Egyptians died, but the ones that belonged to the children of Israel still lived.

Still Pharaoh refused to let the people go!

SIX: THE PLAGUE OF THE BOILS

EXODUS 9

Now the Lord God told Moses and Aaron, "Take handfuls of ashes from a furnace and throw them towards heaven when the Pharaoh is watching. The ashes shall become fine dust throughout Egypt and all whom the dust shall touch, man or animal, shall break out in painful boils."

Moses and Aaron did as the Lord said and even the magicians could not use their magic because they were in such pain from the boils, but the Pharaoh still refused to let the children of Israel leave!

SEVEN: THE PLAGUE OF HAIL AND FIRE

EXODUS 9

"Tomorrow," the Lord told the Pharaoh through Moses and Aaron, "about this time I will make it hail and rain as it never has before in Egypt. Therefore, gather all that you have in your fields and bring it home, for every man who is still in the fields and all things growing on them shall die."

Some Egyptians now feared the word of the Lord and brought their servants and their cattle into their houses, but those who did not believe the word of the Lord left their servants and cattle in the fields and the next day God made Moses raise his rod towards the sky and it began to thunder and hail, and lightning struck the ground. Nothing like it had ever been seen before! And all those in the fields died.

The Pharaoh sent for Moses and Aaron. "It is enough!" he cried. "The Lord is just and I am wicked! Pray to the Lord to stop the thunder and the hail and the lightning and I will let your people go!"

Moses prayed to the Lord and the lightning and hail and thunder stopped, but when the Pharaoh saw this he sinned again and still would not let the children of Israel go!

EIGHT: THE PLAGUE OF THE LOCUSTS

EXODUS 10

"I have let all these things happen," the Lord told Moses, "so that you may tell your son and your son's son what I have done in Egypt and you will know *I am the Lord*. You will now tell the Pharaoh that if he still refuses to let My people go, the next day Egypt shall be covered with locusts and they shall eat everything left to eat."

Moses and Aaron told the Pharaoh this and Pharaoh's servants begged him to let these people leave Egypt so that Egypt would not be destroyed.

"But," said the Pharaoh, "I will not let your children go. Only your men."

Then the Lord caused an east wind to blow over the land all that day and all that night, and when it was morning the east wind brought locusts and the locusts covered the land of Egypt and the land was black with them and they ate every plant and all the fruit from the trees. Not one green thing was left.

Pharaoh summoned Moses and Aaron as quickly as he could!

"Forgive me, I beg you! Pray to your Lord to end this terrible plague!"

Moses and Aaron left the Pharaoh and prayed to the Lord and He sent a strong west wind which blew all the locusts into the sea.

But still the Pharaoh refused to let the children of Israel go!

NINE: THE PLAGUE OF DARKNESS

EXODUS 10

Then the Lord said to Moses, "Stretch out your hand towards the heavens so that there will be a darkness over the land of Egypt so thick it will be felt."

And Moses stretched out his hand towards the heavens and there was a thick darkness throughout the land of Egypt for three days, but the children of Israel had light wherever they lived.

Pharaoh called Moses to him again. "Your people and your children may go if this darkness is lifted from my land but your cattle and your flocks shall be left behind," he said.

Moses refused to leave behind one animal and the Pharaoh said to him, "Leave my presence! Make sure I never see your face again, for if I do I shall have you killed!"

"You have spoken well, O Pharaoh," Moses replied. "You shall never see me again."

TEN: THE PLAGUE OF THE FIRST BORN

EXODUS 11

The Lord told Moses, "I will bring one more plague upon the Pharaoh and upon Egypt. Afterwards he will ask you to leave altogether. Talk to the people, for you are very great in the eyes of Pharaoh's servants and in the eyes of the people."

So Moses told the people as the Lord had said: "About midnight I will come among you and all the first born in the land of Egypt shall die, from the Pharaoh's first born to all the animals in Egypt, but not one child of Israel shall die. You will know then that the Lord has favoured the children of Israel! All who follow the Pharaoh will soon bow down to me!"

But the Pharaoh still would not let the children of Israel go out of his land.

THE TIME OF THE PASSOVER

EXODUS 12

The Lord then told Moses, "Tell all the children of Israel that this month shall be the first month of the year for them and on the tenth day of this month they shall take a lamb from their flocks and keep it until the fourteenth day of the month and then, when all are gathered together, kill the lamb. Then you are to take the lamb's blood and make a mark with it on the sides of your front doors and three marks over your front doors. Then roast the lamb and eat it with unleavened bread and bitter herbs. You shall eat until nothing is left for the morning and you shall eat in haste, ready to leave. It is the Lord's passover. For I will pass through the land of Egypt this night and in the morning all the first born of the Egyptians shall be dead, but where I see blood on a house I shall pass over and the plague shall not touch you, and from this day forth this day shall be a holy day and you shall keep it as a feast to the Lord for ever. For seven days you will eat unleavened bread and on the first and last days you shall hold a holy service and no work shall be done. You will keep this holy day to remember that on this day I brought your people out of the land of Egypt."

Moses called together all the older people of the children of Israel and told them as well, "When you reach the land which the Lord has promised you, you will keep these holy days as long as any child of Israel lives. And when your children ask you, 'What do these holy days mean?' you shall say, 'They are our sacrifice to the Lord for passing over the houses of the children of Israel when He plagued the Egyptians and led us out of slavery'."

The children of Israel went home and did as the Lord God had told them to do and at midnight He passed through the land, but *over* the houses of the children of Israel, and when Pharaoh woke up during the night there was not one house which belonged to an Egyptian that did not have someone who had died that night.

Pharaoh then called Aaron and Moses to him. "Go," he told them, "and take your little ones and your flocks and your herds and be gone! And bless me, too!"

So the children of Israel took their bread that was not raised, and tied up their clothes in bundles over their shoulders and left Egypt and travelled from Rameses to Succoth. There were six hundred thousand of them, not including the children, and they travelled on foot with their flocks and their herds of cattle.

That first night of the Passover ended four hundred and thirty years that the children of Israel had been living in slavery in Egypt.

MOSES CROSSES THE RED SEA

EXODUS 13-14

The children of Israel continued their journey from Succoth. The Lord led them by day as a pillar of cloud and by night as a pillar of fire, and so they had light both day and night.

Now the Egyptians spoke to the Pharaoh. Without

the children of Israel to serve them they had to do
their own work, which did not please them. The
Pharaoh chose six hundred of the finest chariots in
all Egypt and put captains over all of them. Then
they followed the children of Israel until they overtook

Moses and his followers beside the Red Sea. The children of Israel were very frightened and they said to Moses, "Why have you led us into the wilderness to die? It would have been better for us to serve the Egyptians."

"Do not be afraid," Moses assured them. "This will be the last time you will see the Egyptians. The Lord will show us the way."

Then God spoke to Moses: "Lift up your rod and stretch your hand over the sea. The sea will part in two and in the middle there shall be dry land for the children of Israel to cross to the other side."

Then the pillar of cloud in which the Lord had led the children of Israel moved until it was behind them and separated the Egyptians from them so that they could not be seen, because although it was a cloud of light for Moses' followers it was a cloud of darkness for Pharaohs'!

Then Moses stretched out his hand over the sea and the Lord made a strong east wind push the sea back and by morning the sea had parted and the children of Israel crossed over on dry ground. But the Egyptians followed them.

Then the Lord told Moses, "Now stretch out your hand over the waters and the sea will be one water again," and Moses did and the waters returned and covered the chariots and the horsemen. *There was not one left!*

Thus the Lord saved the children of Israel.

MIRIAM'S SONG

EXODUS 15

And Miriam, who was Aaron's sister, took a tambourine and all the other women joined her and they played the tambourines and danced and Miriam sang:

"Sing to the Lord!
He led us through the Red Sea!
And drowned the Pharaoh's men
And triumped gloriously!"

THE BITTER AND THE SWEET WATERS

EXODUS 15

The children of Israel travelled on into the wilderness for three days after crossing the Red Sea and they found no water. When they came to a place where there was water they could not drink it because it was bitter and they called this place Marah, which means "bitter."

"What shall we drink?" the people asked Moses.

And the Lord showed Moses a tree and when the tree had been thrown into the water the water was sweet and they could drink it.

And the Lord told them, "If you will listen to *My* voice and carry out *My* commands, you will never have the plagues I brought upon the Egyptians."

They came next to a place called Elim, where there were twelve wells of sweet water and seventy palm trees, and they camped there.

THE PEOPLE FIND MANNA

EXODUS 16

The children of Israel journeyed into the wilderness and six weeks passed and they now had no food, and they cried to Moses, "You have brought us into the wilderness to die of hunger!"

But the Lord told Moses, "I will rain bread from heaven for you and the people shall go out and gather a certain amount each day and on the sixth day they shall prepare what they bring in and it shall be twice as much as they gather daily. In the evening you shall eat meat and in the morning you shall have your fill of bread and you shall know that I am the Lord your God."

That evening, birds flew over the camp and they ate the meat and in the morning a dew covered the ground and when the dew was gone they saw small white pieces on the ground that they called manna, which Moses told them was bread. They gathered the bread. Some took more and some took less but when they measured it they all had the same amount! On the sixth day they gathered twice as much bread and came to Moses and praised what had happened.

"This is what the Lord has said," he told them. "Tomorrow you shall rest and not work. It will be the Holy Sabbath. Take what you gathered today and bake it all so that you will have it to eat tomorrow. For six days you shall gather bread but on the seventh day there will be none."

But there were some who went out on the seventh day and found none!

THE SABBATH

"How long will you refuse to obey what I say?" the Lord asked Moses. "The Lord has given you on the sixth day enough bread for two days. No man shall go out on the seventh day which is the Sabbath."

So the people rested on the Sabbath and ate the manna which was white and tasted like biscuits made with honey.

THE WATER FROM THE ROCK

And the children of Israel travelled on and came next to Rephidim, where they pitched their tents. But there was no water to drink.

"Give us water!" the people shouted at Moses.

And Moses asked the Lord, "What shall I do? The people are ready to stone me."

"Go before the people with your rod and let them follow you to the river. There will be the rock of Horeb there and you shall strike it with your rod and water will pour out of it for the people to drink."

And Moses did as the Lord said and the people had water to drink.

THE WAR WITH AMALEK

While the children of Israel were in Rephidim an army led by a man named Amalek attacked them. Moses spoke to Joshua and told him, "Choose men to fight Amalek and tomorrow I will stand on top of the hill with the rod of God in my hand."

Joshua did as Moses asked and went out with the men he had picked to fight Amalek, and Moses, Aaron and Hur went to the top of the hill. There Moses held up his hand and when he did Joshua and his men were winning but when he lowered his hand Amalek moved forward. Moses' hands were heavy and it was difficult for him to keep them in that position and so they took a stone and made him sit on it, and with Aaron on one side and Hur on the other they held up his hands so that by sundown Amalek's army was beaten.

JETHRO AND MOSES

Moses' father-in-law, Jethro, heard of all God had done for Moses and the children of Israel and he came out into the wilderness to see Moses and his daughter and his two grandsons and Moses went to meet him and brought him back to his tent.

The next day Jethro saw how the people stood by Moses from morning until evening.

"Why do you sit here alone?" he asked Moses. "And why do the people stand here from morning until evening?"

"They come to me when they have a matter that needs settling and I listen and inquire of God and then tell them what God's law is," Moses told him.

"That is too big a burden for one man," his father-in-law told him. "I will tell you what I think. Choose from your people able men who fear God, men of truth and honesty. Let there be rulers of thousands and rulers of hundreds and rulers of tens. They shall judge for the people in small matters but if a matter is great then they shall come to you. This way your burden will be shared."

Moses listened to his father-in-law and did as he said. Then Jethro went back to his own land.

MOSES ON MOUNT SINAI

EXODUS 19

The children of Israel travelled on until they came to the wilderness of Sinai. And the Lord called Moses to the mountain.

"You shall obey my voice and keep your agreement with me and then you shall be a chosen people."

"All that the Lord asks we will do," the people told Moses.

God was pleased and called Moses again to Mount Sinai. "I will come in a thick cloud so that the people will hear my words as you do and believe you for ever. Go now and let the people wash their clothes and be ready for the third day, for I shall come down in sight of all the people upon Mount Sinai. The people must be warned that they cannot go up the mountain or touch it. Anyone who does so will be killed. When the trumpet sounds they shall come up to Mount Sinai."

The morning of the third day there was thunder and lightning and a thick cloud lay upon the mountain. A trumpet blasted so loud that all the people trembled.

Moses led the people to the foot of the mountain. Mount Sinai was covered with smoke. The smoke rose up and the whole mountain trembled and shook.

The trumpet grew louder and louder and Moses spoke to God and God answered him. Then the Lord came down upon the top of Mount Sinai and He called Moses up to the top of the mountain and Moses went.

THE TEN COMMANDMENTS

EXODUS 20

And then God spoke all these words: "I am the Lord God who brought you out of the land of Egypt and out of slavery and these are My ten commandments:

1. You shall have no other gods but Me.

2. You shall not make any statues or any likenesses of anything that is in heaven above or on the earth beneath, or in the water under the earth.

3. You shall not bow down to them or serve them, for I am a jealous God who will punish the children of those who hate Me and show mercy to those who love Me and keep My commandments.

4. You shall not take the name of the Lord your God in vain.

5. Remember the Sabbath Day and keep it holy.

6. Honour your father and your mother.

7. You shall not kill.

8. You shall not commit adultery.

9. You shall not steal.

10. You shall not wrongly accuse a neighbour nor envy a neighbour's wife or his servants or his animals or anything that is your neighbour's.

The people heard the thunderings and the sound of the trumpet and saw the lightnings and the mountain smoking and they stood back and they said to Moses, "You speak to us and we will listen, but we may die if we listen to God!"

"Don't be frightened," Moses told them. "God is just testing you so that you will learn to respect Him and won't do wrong."

The people stood far off but Moses went closer and into the darkness where God was.

THE ANGEL OF GOD

EXODUS 23

God also told the people, "You shall have three feasts a year to Me; the feast of the unleavened bread, the feast of the harvest and the feast of the in-gathering when all the harvests have been gathered, and three times a year all your males shall appear before the Lord.

"I shall send an Angel before you to show you the way to the place I have prepared for you. Beware of him and obey him for he will not forgive your sins. But if you do indeed obey him then I will be an enemy to your enemies and a friend to your friends.

"You shall serve the Lord and He shall bless your bread and your water and take sickness away.

"I will not drive out the people of the lands you are going to because the land may grow bare and the animals multiply and turn against you. But little by little I shall drive them out and your families will increase and you will inherit the land."

THE LORD'S ARK

EXODUS 24-31

Moses wrote down all the words of the Lord and the people said, "All the Lord has said we will do."

Then God said to Moses, "Come up to Me in the mountain and I will give you tablets of stone with the law and the commandments on them so that you can teach them."

Moses and his minister, Joshua, went into the mountain of God and when Moses went to the mountain a cloud covered it for six days. Moses went into the cloud and remained on the mountain for forty days and forty nights.

God told Moses, "The people of Israel shall make Me an ark of acacia wood. It shall be a chest four feet long, two feet wide and two feet high. It is to be covered with gold inside and out and it shall have gold rings and through these rings shall be passed gold-covered rods of acacia wood so that the ark may

be carried. Inside the ark shall be placed the laws I gave you.

"Then the people shall make Me a throne of pure gold, four feet long and two feet wide: At each end there shall be the figure of an Angel and the Angels shall stretch their wings upward covering the throne with them. They shall face one another and they shall be looking down and the throne shall be placed on top of the ark.

"Then they shall make a table of acacia wood and cover it with gold and put a gold band around it with gold rings at each corner. And then they shall make a candlestick of pure gold with three branches on either side so that there shall be a place for seven candles.

"Then you will have the people put up a tent lined with fine linen and with blue and purple and scarlet cloth and the ark and the throne shall be kept in here and covered with a curtain of blue and purple and scarlet cloth.

"Every Sabbath twelve loaves of bread shall be placed there to be eaten by the priests. And the people of Israel shall make an altar and set it up before the tent.

"Aaron and his sons shall become My priests. You shall make holy garments for Aaron for glory and beauty: a breastplate, a shawl, a robe, an embroidered coat, a turban and a belt. The shawl shall be made of gold and blue and purple and scarlet linen. The breastplate shall have chains of pure gold and another gold plate engraved with the words *Holiness to the Lord* shall be put in the front of his turban and worn on his forehead. Aaron must wear this plate at all times and he and his sons shall be made priests."

And when God had finished talking to Moses upon Mount Sinai He gave him two tablets of the law and the commandments written in the hand of the Lord.

THE GOLDEN CALF

When the people saw that Moses was not coming down from the mountain they gathered around Aaron and said to him, "Make us gods for we do not know what has become of Moses."

Aaron told them to bring all their golden ear-rings from their wives and daughters to him and they did and Aaron melted the gold into a golden calf.

"Let this be your god," he said. Then he made an altar before it and told the people: "Tomorrow is a feast day to the Lord, the Golden Calf."

The people got up early in the morning and brought offerings to the golden calf; then they ate and drank and danced.

God told Moses, "Go, for your people have sinned and broken one of My commandments!"

And though the Lord was hot with anger, Moses spoke to Him and He relented and did not turn His anger on the people.

THE END OF THE GOLDEN CALF

EXODUS 32

Moses went down the mountain and carried the two tablets of the laws written in God's hand. When Joshua heard the people's loud voices he said, "There is war in the camp."

"Not war," Moses told him, "but the sound of singing."

As soon as Moses came near the camp he saw the calf and the dancing and he grew angry and threw the tablets from his hands and they broke. Then he took the calf they had made and burnt it in the fire and ground it to powder and stirred it into the water and made the people of Israel drink it!

The next day Moses said to the people, "You have sinned badly. Now I will go up to the Lord. Perhaps I can get Him to forgive you."

When Moses spoke to the Lord the Lord told him, "Go, lead the people to the place I have told you. My Angel shall go before you. The time shall come when I shall punish the people for their sin."

A RENEWED PROMISE

EXODUS 34-40

God said to Moses, "Take two tablets of stone like the first and I will write upon these tablets the words that were on them when you broke the tablets. Come up in the morning to Mount Sinai and stand there before Me at the top of the mountain, and you must come alone."

So Moses cut two tablets of stone like the first and rose early in the morning and went up Mount Sinai as the Lord had commanded, holding the two tablets of stone. God came down in the cloud and stood with him there.

God said, "I will make a promise. I will do wonders for all your people as have never been done elsewhere before. All your people shall see the work of the Lord. But you must keep all My commandments and worship Me according to My laws."

Moses stayed with the Lord for forty days and forty nights and he did not eat or drink during this time, and he wrote the ten commandments and the words of the law on the tablets.

When Moses came down from Mount Sinai with the tablets his face was shining so brightly that the children of Israel were afraid to come close to him. Moses put a veil over his face and spoke, telling them what the Lord had said; then he took off the veil and the children of Israel looked upon his shining face.

The children of Israel then made all the things that the Lord had commanded. They raised the tent for the ark and the Lord covered it with a cloud when they were to rest and removed it when they continued their journey.

NUMBERS

THE PRINCES OF ISRAEL

The Lord spoke to Moses in the wilderness of Sinai and He said, "Take all the male children of Israel from twenty years of age on, all that are able to fight for Israel, and number them. There shall be twelve tribes from the twelve sons of Israel, and twelve princes, each one named for Israel's sons. They shall be:

"The Tribe of Reuben with Elizur as prince.
The Tribe of Simeon with Shelumiel as prince.
The Tribe of Judah with Nahshon as prince.
The Tribe of Issachar with Nethaneel as prince.
The Tribe of Zebulun with Eliab as prince.
The Tribe of Joseph with Elishama as prince.
The Tribe of Manasseh with Gamaliel as prince.

The Tribe of Benjamin with Abidan as prince.
The Tribe of Dan with Ahiezer as prince.
The Tribe of Asher with Pagiel as prince.
The Tribe of Gad with Eliasaph as prince.
The Tribe of Naphtali with Ahira as prince."
But the Lord asked Moses not to number the tribe of the Levites. Instead they became the guards of the Holy Tent, carrying it with them wherever the children of Israel travelled. They were to pitch it and take it down and any stranger who interfered would be put to death.

THE GREAT CLOUD

NUMBERS 9

The children of Israel continued their journey. A cloud covered the Holy Tent during the daytime and a fire burned beside it at night, but they would not move on until the cloud lifted and moved before them even if it remained for two days, or a month, or a year.

THE SILVER TRUMPETS

The Lord told Moses, "Make two trumpets of silver and when you blow them both all the people shall come together, but if you blow just one then the twelve princes of Israel shall gather before you.

"The sons of Aaron, the priests, shall blow the trumpets and if you should go to war against an enemy they shall blow an alarm and I will hear it and come to help you."

MIRIAM'S PUNISHMENT

NUMBERS 12

Miriam and Aaron spoke against Moses because he had married an Ethiopian woman different from them, and the Lord heard them and was very angry.

The cloud lifted from the tent and when Moses and Aaron looked at Miriam her skin was covered with sores. Moses begged the Lord to heal Miriam and forgive her. The Lord answered, "Shut her out of the camp for seven days and after that she may join you again."

Miriam was shut out of the camp and the people did not move onward until she was with them again.

THE TWELVE SPIES

NUMBERS 13

When they had reached Paran, near the land of Canaan, Moses chose twelve men, one from each of the tribes of Israel, to go to the land of Canaan as spies.

"Go up into the mountains," He told them, "and look over the land to see what it is like. Find out if the people who live there are weak or strong and how many there are. See whether the earth is rich or not. See if there are trees—and bring back the fruit of the land."

The twelve spies went out and searched the land ahead of them. They came to a brook and there they cut down a branch with a cluster of grapes on it. As they went on they picked pomegranates and figs. When they returned to Moses and Aaron and the children of Israel they showed them the fruit.

"It is indeed a land of milk and honey," they said, "yet the people are strong and the cities are walled and very large. We saw the children of Anak there. To the south are the Amalekites; in the mountains are the Hittites, the Jehusites and the Amorites, and the Canaanites have the land by the sea and along the river Jordan."

Caleb, who had been one of the twelve spies, said, "Let us go at once and take possession of the land. We are strong enough!"

But some of the others said, "We are not able to fight these people! You are wrong. They are stronger than we and the land is a land that eats up the people who live there. All the people are huge. The sons of Anak are giants! We looked like grasshoppers beside them!"

JOSHUA AND CALEB SPEAK

NUMBERS 14

Then all the people lifted up their voices and cried. They turned against Moses and Aaron. "Let us choose a new leader and let us return to Egypt!" they shouted.

Caleb and Joshua, who had been two of the twelve spies, spoke to the people. "The land we went through," they said, "is good land. If the Lord is pleased with us and gives it to us it will truly be a land flowing with milk and honey. But do not go against the Lord and do not fear the people of the land. The Lord is with us."

But the people nearly threw stones at Caleb and Joshua and God grew very angry and spoke to Moses.

"How long will these people do things to make me angry?" He said. "How long will it be before they believe in Me and the signs I show them? If they continue like this, I will strike them with a plague and disinherit them and make a great nation of *you* alone!"

THE UPRISING

NUMBERS 16

Now Korah, the son of Izhar, and Dothan and Abiram, the sons of Eliah, and On, the son of Paleth, rose up against Moses with two hundred and fifty princes of the people; all famous and respected men.

"You take too much upon yourselves," they told Moses and Aaron. "Since all the people have God among them and are holy why should you be above everyone else?"

Moses spoke to Korah and his men, "Tomorrow the Lord will show you who is holy. Each man take an incense burner and light it and place it before the

Lord; *all two hundred and fifty of you and Aaron and myself.*"

The next day all the two hundred and fifty princes brought their lighted incense burners to the Holy Tent and the Lord appeared before them. He spoke to Moses and Aaron.

"Leave this place," He told them, "so that you may not be injured when I set fire to it and the rest are killed."

The two hundred and fifty princes fell immediately upon their faces. "O God!" they cried. "Don't blame all of us. Spare some!"

And the Lord spared all but the four leaders.

THE TWELVE RODS

NUMBERS 17-18

The Lord told Moses, "Talk to the children of Israel and have each tribe give you a rod and on each of the twelve rods write one man's name. The man's rod which I shall choose shall blossom."

Moses collected all the rods and placed them before the Lord in the Holy Tent. The next morning the rod of Aaron for the house of Levi had buds and blossoms and almonds on it. Moses brought out all the rods to show the children of Israel and every man took back his own rod, for the Lord had separated Aaron and his brother, Moses, from the rest.

THE WATER AND THE ROCK

The children of Israel wandered into the desert of Sin. They stopped at Kadish, where Miriam died and was buried. Once again there was no water and God spoke to Moses.

"You and Aaron take the rod and gather the people together. Speak to the rock while the people watch. Soon it shall sprout water enough for all the people and their cattle to drink."

So Moses gathered all the people together before the rock and said to them, "I shall bring water out of this rock." Then he raised his hand and struck the rock twice with his rod and the water came flowing out.

KING EDOM

Moses sent messengers from Kadish to the King of Edom and said to him, "We the people of Israel are at your borders. Let us pass, I beg you. We will not tramp through your fields or drink from your wells. We will not turn right or left until we have passed the far borders of your country."

But King Edom would not let them pass.

AARON DIES

The people went instead to Mount Hor and there on the top of the mountain Aaron died and his son, Eleazar, put on his priest's robes and came down the mountain with Moses. And when the people heard Aaron had died they mourned him for thirty days.

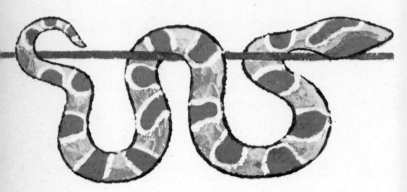

THE BRASS SERPENT

In order to go around the land of Edom, the children of Israel travelled from Mount Hor by way of the Red Sea. But the people were very discouraged and spoke against the Lord and the Lord sent fierce serpents among the people. The people came to Moses and begged him to ask the Lord to take the serpents away and Moses told them, "Make a serpent of brass and put it on a pole. Everyone who has been bitten by a serpent shall live if he looks upon it."

This had been God's command, so when the pole was made those who had been bitten by a serpent looked at the brass serpent and they lived.

THE SONG OF THE WELL

NUMBERS 21

The people went to Beer, near the country of the Amorites. There was a well at Beer and God told Moses to gather the people and He would give them all water. They gathered together and they all sang this song:

> "Spring up, O well,
>   We are singing to you.
> Hear our bell—
> Spring up, O well!"

And the princes and the nobles dug and they had plenty of water.

THE AMORITES

NUMBERS 21

Then they sent messengers to Sihon, the King of the Amorites. "Let us pass through your land. We will not walk over your fields or into your vineyards. We will not drink the waters from your wells. We will keep to ourselves until we have passed your borders."

But King Sihon would not let them go through his country and instead gathered his men together and went out to fight the children of Israel. It was a fierce battle and the children of Israel used their swords well and won and took over the Amorites' cities and villages.

THE KING OF BASHAN

NUMBERS 21

Then a neighbouring country called Bashan, whose king's name was Og, decided to fight the children of Israel who now lived in the land of the Amorites.

The Lord said to Moses, "Do not fear King Og. I have delivered him into your hand. You will win the land of Bashan as you did the land of the Amorites."

The children of Israel and the armies of Bashan fought and it was such a fierce battle that not one follower of King Og remained alive at the end of it, and so the children of Israel had his land, too.

KING BALEK SENDS MESSENGERS

NUMBERS 22

Time passed and the children of Israel were living in the plains of Moab, on the side of the river Jordan near Jericho. King Balek was a neighbouring king and, knowing what the children of Israel did to the land of Bashan and the land of the Amorites, was frightened that the children of Israel would take over his country as well. Therefore, he sent messengers to King Balaam who was his neighbour and said to him, "There is a tribe of people that has come from Egypt and soon they will conquer the world if we don't stop them. Join with me to fight them for they are too many and too strong for me."

King Balaam gave the messengers lodging for the night and told them he would speak to God.

"What men are these to whom you have given lodging?" the Lord asked King Balaam.

"Messengers of King Balek, who wants me to join with him and fight against these people from Egypt," King Balaam told the Lord.

"You shall not fight them for I have blessed them," the Lord told him.

The next morning King Balaam told King Balek's messengers, "Go back to your king and tell him, 'The Lord refuses to let me fight these people because He has blessed them.'"

KING BALEK SENDS HIS PRINCES

NUMBERS 22

King Balek's messengers went back and told their king what King Balaam had said. King Balek then sent princes more esteemed than the messengers. The princes went to King Balaam.

"Our king will do anything you say. He will give you great honours if you will help him fight these people."

And King Balaam told them, "If your king gave me his house full of silver and gold I could not go against what the Lord tells me. But you may spend the night here."

But King Balaam rose in the morning and saddled his donkey and went with King Balek's princes.

THE ANGEL BARS KING BALAAM'S WAY

NUMBERS 22

God was very angry because King Balaam went and he sent an Angel who stood and barred King Balaam's way. The donkey saw the Angel of the Lord with his sword drawn and the donkey moved out of the way and into a field. King Balaam whipped the donkey to go back on the road but the Angel now stood in the fields before them and there was a wall to one side.

When the donkey saw the Angel again he became frightened and started forward and rammed into the wall and crushed King Balaam's foot. Still King Balaam whipped the donkey to continue.

Then the Angel of the Lord went farther and stood in a narrow place so that King Balaam on the donkey could not turn either to the left nor to the right. Thereupon the donkey grew more frightened and fell to the ground. King Balaam tumbled after him. The king got up and whipped the donkey to rise, but the Lord put words into the donkey's mouth.

"Why have you whipped me three times?" the donkey asked.

"Because you have made a fool of me and if I had a sword I would kill you!" King Balaam told the donkey.

"Am I not the same donkey you have always ridden? Have I not always before done as you commanded?"

Then the Angel of the Lord again stood before them. When Balaam saw the Angel he bowed his head and fell flat on his face.

THE ANGEL AND KING BALAAM

NUMBERS 22

The Angel said to King Balaam, "Why have you whipped your donkey three times? If she had not turned from me I would have slain you and saved her."

"I have sinned," King Balaam confessed. "I shall return to my own country."

"No. Go with the men," the Angel told him. "But you shall only say what I shall tell you."

And King Balaam agreed and went on with the princes of King Balek.

KING BALAAM'S PROPHECY

NUMBERS 23-24

King Balaam told King Balek that the Lord now spoke for him. King Balek took him to the top of his tallest mountain and showed him his land and his people below. Then King Balaam spoke to the Lord and when he returned to King Balek he blessed the children of Israel.

King Balek was very angry! "I called you to fight our enemies and you bless them. Go back to your own country!"

"I told your messengers I must do as the Lord says. I will tell you what the children of Israel will do to your nation. The Lord says, 'There shall come a star out of Jacob, and a sceptre shall rise out of Israel and shall destroy your land and strike down your children and conquer your country and a child of Jacob's shall become a man of great power and he shall destroy all that remains of your cities.'"

Then King Balaam rose and returned to his own country and King Balek also went his own way.

THE LAW OF INHERITANCE

NUMBERS 27

After many years Joseph's tribe no longer had any men to pass on their name, as only girls had been born to them. All the daughters of that tribe came before Moses.

"Our father died in the wilderness," they told him. "Why should the name of his family be lost because there are no longer any sons? Give us an inheritance in our father's name."

Moses spoke to the Lord and the Lord told him, "From here on if a man dies and has no sons then his inheritance shall pass on to his daughters, and if he has no daughters it shall go to his brothers; and if he should have no brothers, to his father's brothers. And if his father should have no brothers, then to the next relation."

THE MARRIAGE OF THE HEIRESSES

NUMBERS 36

Moses, speaking for the Lord, told the daughters of Joseph's tribe that they could marry whom they thought best, but only to members of their father's tribe.

"So shall the inheritance," Moses said, "of the children of Israel not be removed from one tribe to another."

138

DEUTERONOMY

THE SONG OF MOSES

DEUTERONOMY 32

When Moses was one hundred and twenty years old and the children of Israel had been wandering for forty years in search of the Promised Land, the Lord called Moses and Joshua to him and He taught Moses a song for him to bring back to the people:

> "Listen and I will speak.
> Listen to my words.
> They shall fall like small showers
> Upon the tender grass.
>
> As an eagle stirs up her nest,
> Flutters over her young,
> Spreads out her wings, takes them,
> Carries them on her wings—
>
> So the Lord alone leads Israel."

MOSES SEES CANAAN

Then Moses climbed to the top of Mount Nebo and the Lord showed him all the land he was giving to each of the tribes of Israel.

"This is the land which I promised your fathers. I have let you see it with your own eyes before you die," the Lord told Moses.

After Moses died, the people turned to Joshua, who was wise and good. But they mourned Moses for a long time. Never again in Israel was there a man like Moses who spoke to the Lord face to face and who did all the magic and wonders which Moses did in the name of the Lord.

JOSHUA

GOD'S WORDS TO JOSHUA

After the death of Moses God told Joshua, "You shall lead the people. Every place you walk shall be yours, from the wilderness to the great river, to the greater sea and as far as the horizon. And I shall always be with you. Be strong and very courageous and observe the laws and commandments and you will be safe and successful. Your wives and your little ones and your cattle shall remain this side of Jordan but you will gather all the brave men and go onward."

And Joshua came down from the mountain and told the people what the Lord had said to him and the people accepted Joshua as their leader.

THE TWO SPIES AND RAHAB

JOSHUA 2

Joshua sent two spies to Jericho. They stopped at the house of a woman named Rahab. The King of Jericho was warned of their arrival and sent his men to her house.

"Where are the spies?" the men asked.

"There were two men who came here," Rahab replied. "However, they left when night came. I don't know where they were going but since they have only left a short time ago if you hurry you may overtake them."

But Rahab was not telling the truth, for she had taken the two spies up to the roof of her house and hidden them there. The king's men searched for the spies all the way to the river Jordan but could not find them.

Then Rahab told the two spies, "I know that the Lord has given you this land. All the people here fear you for that reason. They heard how the Lord dried up the waters of the Red Sea for you. For my kindness I ask you to promise no harm shall come to my father and my mother and my brothers and sisters and their families."

"When the Lord has given us this land," the spies said, "we will deal kindly with you."

THE SPIES ESCAPE

JOSHUA 2

Rahab helped the spies escape. Before she left them she said, "Go to the mountains and hide there for three days. Then go on your way."

The men told Rahab, "When the children of Israel come into your land you must tie a piece of scarlet ribbon to your window and bring all your family into your house. They shall all be safe unless you say a word about our business here."

"Not one word," Rahab said, and as soon as the two spies were out of sight she tied the piece of scarlet ribbon to the window.

THE SPIES RETURN

JOSHUA 2

The two spies went to the mountains and stayed there for three days while the king's men searched unsuccessfully for them and finally gave up the hunt and went back to the city. Then the two men came down from the mountain and crossed the river and returned to Joshua.

"What did you find?" Joshua asked.

"The people all faint with fear at the thought of us," the men told him.

THE PARTING OF THE WATERS OF THE JORDAN

The people moved towards Jericho. The priests went first carrying the ark. As they came to the shores of the river Jordan, which had overflowed on to the banks because it was harvest-time, the waters stopped flowing and rose up like a wall on each side. The priests and the people passed over on dry ground and the river Jordan did not flow again until the last child of Israel had passed.

THE LORD'S CAPTAIN

When Joshua and the children of Israel were near Jericho, Joshua looked up to the sky and there, above him, stood a man with a sword in his hand.

"Are you friend or enemy?" Joshua asked him.

"I am captain of the host of the Lord come to lead you," the man said.

Joshua fell to the earth on his knees. "What can I do for my lord?" Joshua asked.

"First take off your shoes, for the place you rest upon is holy."

And Joshua did as the man said and the man led him forward.

THE WALLS OF JERICHO FALL

JOSHUA 6

Jericho, that great city, was kept carefully guarded. The people knew the children of Israel would come; therefore, no one went out of the city and no one came in.

The Lord had told Joshua how to capture the city and Joshua told his people. "The priests," he said, "shall carry the ark. Seven more priests shall march before them carrying seven trumpets made from rams' horns. The rest of you shall surround the city. Those who are armed will go first. You shall march silently; no sound, even on the rams' horns. And then I shall tell you to shout and to blow the horns."

Early the next morning they circled the city and when Joshua told them to blow the horns and shout they did so. Then they returned to their camp. They did this for six days. On the seventh day the people in Jericho heard the sound of the trumpets and the great shouts. The walls of Jericho came tumbling down. The people of Israel walked into the city and took command.

154

RAHAB'S RESCUE

JOSHUA 6

Joshua told the two men who had spied for him in Jericho to go to Rahab's house and bring out Rahab and her family. The two spies did and then took Rahab and her family outside the fallen city and into the camp of the Israelites.

Joshua saved Rahab's life and her father's household and all that she had. He did this because she had hidden the messengers he had sent to spy on the city of Jericho.

THE CAPTURE OF AI

JOSHUA 8

The Lord told Joshua to take all his brave men and conquer the city of Ai which was near Jericho. Joshua chose thirty thousand mighty men and sent them into the night with orders that they should wait not far from Ai and be ready when the rest of the children of Israel approached the city. Then, when the people of Ai would have seen them, they were to turn and run as if frightened of the people of Ai. The people of Ai in turn would come after them. Then when the people of Ai were away from their city, they would turn and fight them to the man and march in and take the city.

And it happened just as Joshua said it would.

THE TATTERED MESSENGERS

JOSHUA 9

The people of Gibeon, not far from Ai, heard what Joshua had done to Ai and to Jericho. But they thought that if Joshua believed them to be a poor country he would not harm them. So they sent messengers dressed in tatters who carried only stale bread in their packs.

The messengers came to Joshua in his camp.

"Who are you and where do you come from?" Joshua asked.

"We have come from a distant country and we are a poor people," the messengers replied.

Joshua looked at the tattered men and without asking the Lord's advice drew up a paper that would mean the children of Israel would not fight these poor people and swore a solemn oath to keep it. But three days later he learned the truth, for when the children of Israel reached Gibeon they saw what a rich city it was, but they would not fight because they had sworn a solemn oath.

THE FIVE KINGS

When the King of Jerusalem heard that Joshua had made peace with the people of Gibeon he was much afraid, because Gibeon was a rich and royal city and its men were famous for their bravery. So he called together four other kings from nearby cities to join with him to attack Gibeon.

The people in Gibeon sent a message to Joshua who was in his camp outside the city, saying, "Come quickly and save us, for five kings who live nearby have joined together against us."

Joshua and his army met the five smaller armies before they reached the city of Gibeon and they fought a fierce battle and Joshua won. And as the armies fled the Lord sent hailstones from the skies and the remaining armies of the five kings were struck down.

THE SUN AND THE MOON STAND STILL

Joshua then spoke to the Lord and thanked Him for His help and the Lord told him to speak to the moon and the sun.

"Sun, keep shining on Gibeon so the people can see if an enemy approaches," he said to the sun.

"Moon, stay bright in the valley so that the enemy can be seen even there," Joshua told the moon.

And the moon and the sun both stayed bright until the enemy no longer thought to return.

THE BIG WAR

But now Jabin, King of Hazar, heard about Joshua and he sent messengers to the north and to the south and to the east and the west, to all the kingdoms near him and they all joined together to fight Joshua and the children of Israel. There were more men than sand on the shore and many horses and chariots.

But the Lord told Joshua, "Be not afraid of these people, for tomorrow about this time I will deliver them to you!"

It was a very big war but all the men except the children of Israel were killed that day. So Joshua took all the land and the hills and the south country and all the land of Goshen and the valley and the plain and the mountain of Israel and the valley of Lebanon under Mount Hermon. And then Joshua gave it to the children of Israel who divided it into twelve equal parts for the twelve tribes and the land rested from war.

JOSHUA'S WISE WORDS

JOSHUA 23-24

When Joshua grew very old he called the children of Israel to him and spoke to them.

"You have seen all that the Lord God has done for you," he told them. "You are to be very courageous and keep and do all that is written in the book of law of Moses. This day I am going away but it shall come to pass that good things will come to you. But if you forsake the Lord and serve strange gods He will turn against you and harm you."

"We will serve the Lord!" the people told Joshua.

Then Joshua, who was one hundred and ten years old, closed his eyes and slept for ever on the north side of the hill of Gaash.

JUDGES

THE JUDGES

JUDGES 1

After Joshua died, Judah and Simeon and Man-hasseh and many others divided the rule, but they all did many things that did not please the Lord and He grew very angry. Nevertheless, He gave the children of Israel judges to guide them.

But still they would not listen to the judges and that made the Lord even angrier.

So the children of Israel served many unjust kings for many years.

THE GOLDEN DAGGER

JUDGES 3

The children of Israel had been serving a very unjust king, Eglon of Moab, for eighteen years. They cried to the Lord and He sent them Ehud, from the tribe of Benjamin, to help. Now, Ehud had a golden dagger with two sharp sides and he hid it under his cloak and told the king he had a present to bring him from the children of Israel.

He was brought before the very fat King Eglon. Then Ehud asked the king to order all the people leave before he gave him the present, as it came from God. The king did this and because the king had commanded it everyone left him and Ehud alone.

The king was sitting in his summer throne room and Ehud said, "I shall give you the present from God, now."

The king rose from his throne and as he did Ehud, with his left hand, took the golden dagger from its hiding-place and thrust it into the fat king's stomach. The king was so fat that the dagger disappeared.

Then Ehud left the summer throne room and locked the doors. After he had gone, the king's servants came but when they found the doors locked they thought the king wanted it so and they waited and waited. But when he did not come out they took a key and opened the doors and found the dead king.

But Ehud escaped and joined the children of Israel and they blew the trumpet and then went down the mountain of Ephraim and fought the Moabs and won.

DEBORAH

JUDGES 4

But when Ehud died the children of Israel again went against the word of the Lord and the Lord sold them to Jabin, King of Canaan, whose captain was Sisera and he had nine hundred chariots of iron. For twenty years the cruel Sisera ruled the children of Israel.

Now at this time there was a woman named Deborah whom the Lord had chosen as judge of the children of Israel, and she lived underneath a giant palm tree at the foot of Mount Ephraim and all the children of Israel came to her for judgment.

She sent for Barek, whom she had been watching and knew was good, and told him, "I will cause Sisera, the captain of King Jabin's army, and his chariots and his army to come to you at the river Keshon and you will fight him and win."

But Barek said, "If you will come with me I shall go. But if you will not, I shall not."

"I will go with you," Deborah said and rose and went with Barek and his ten thousand men.

THE BATTLE WITH SISERA

The armies of Barek and Sisera met and the Lord defeated Sisera and his chariots and Barek killed all Sisera's men. Sisera himself got out of his chariot and fled on foot. When he reached Kadesh he stopped at the tent of Heber, who was one of King Jabin's friends. Heber's wife, Jael, came out to meet him.

"Come in," she said. "Do not be afraid."

Sisera went into the tent and Jael made him lie down and covered him with a cloak.

He said, "I am thirsty. Give me some water to drink."

She took a bottle and gave him some milk instead and made him comfortable.

"Stand in the door of the tent," he told her, "and when anybody comes and asks questions say 'Nobody is here.'"

Then Sisera fell asleep and while he slept Jael killed him.

When Barek arrived and said "Is anyone here?" Jael took him inside the tent and showed him the dead Sisera.

The children of Israel conquered Canaan and there was peace for the next forty years.

GIDEON

But once again the children of Israel went against the word of the Lord and the Lord delivered them into the cruel hands of Midian for seven years. But there was a young man named Gideon who threshed wheat in secret for his father to hide from the Midianites and one day while he was doing so an Angel appeared beneath an oak tree near him.

"The Lord is with you," the Angel told Gideon, "for you are a brave and good man."

"If the Lord is with us why are we suffering? Where are His miracles of which our fathers told us?" Gideon asked.

"You shall go tonight and save Israel from the Midianites," the Angel told him.

"But how? My family is poor, and I am the youngest in my father's house," Gideon replied.

"I will be with you," said the Angel.

GIDEON'S FATHER SPEAKS FOR HIM

That night Gideon took ten men and they tore down an altar to Baal, a false god, and in its place made an altar to the Lord God.

The next morning the villagers saw what Gideon had done and the men of Midian went to Gideon's father and said, "Bring out your son. He must die."

But Gideon's father said, "If your god, Baal, wants to put my son to death let him speak for himself."

And there was silence and Gideon was spared.

THE FLEECE

JUDGES 6

The Spirit of the Lord came to Gideon and he blew a trumpet and all the men flocked to his side.. Gideon spoke to the Lord.

"Show me a sign," Gideon asked of the Lord. "I shall put wool fleece on the floor and if the earth is dry and the fleece damp with dew then I will know you mean that I am to save Israel."

Gideon placed the fleece on the ground and left it there for the night. The next morning he rose early and went to where the fleece was and wrung from it a bowl of water, but the earth all around was dry!

Still he doubted. "Do not be angry at me," he asked of the Lord, "but grant me one more sign. Let the fleece be dry and the earth wet."

Again he left some fleece on the dry earth and the next morning the fleece was dry and the earth was wet!

THE THREE HUNDRED MEN

Then Gideon gathered an army together from the men of Israel. They pitched their tents beside the well of Harod, so that the army of the Midianites was off to the north by a hill, but in a valley.

But God told Gideon, "You have too many men. Tell all those you have that anyone who is afraid shall go back and not fight."

Twenty-two thousand men went back but ten thousand stayed with Gideon. "There are still too many men," God told him. "Bring them all down to the water and tell them to drink of it. Separate those who lap the water with their tongues like a dog from those who kneel to drink with their hands."

Gideon brought all the people to the water and told them to drink and of the ten thousand only three hundred lapped the water like a dog.

"Let all but the three hundred go home," God told Gideon. "These three hundred men will help you save Israel."

Gideon sent all the rest of the Israelites to their tents and kept only the three hundred men.

And the army of the Midianites was below them in the valley.

THE DREAM

JUDGES 7-8

Then God told Gideon, "Go down to the camp of the Midianites and listen to what they are saying and, afterwards, your hands will be strong for battle."

Gideon went to the outskirts of the camp. There were so many of the enemy that they could not be counted. Gideon was silent and crept closer and he heard one man tell another a dream.

"I dreamed that a cake of barley bread tumbled into the camp of Midian. It struck a tent and the tent overturned," the man said.

His companion told him, "That is the sword of Gideon! God is going to let him win over us!"

Gideon went back to his men. He divided the three hundred men into three companies and he placed a trumpet in every man's hand and gave each one an empty pitcher with a light inside it.

"Watch me and do as I do," he told them. "When we come to the edge of the camp, blow your trumpets on every side of the camp and shout, 'The sword of the Lord and of Gideon!'"

When they did this the enemy fled. Then the men of Israel asked Gideon to rule over them. There was peace while Gideon lived and then the children of Israel forgot the word of the law and the goodness of Gideon. And his own sons fought between them.

SAMSON

JUDGES 13-14

For forty years the people of Israel were slaves to the Philistines. During this time there was a man named Manoah and he had no children. The Angel of the Lord appeared to his wife and told her that she was to have a son. "But," the Angel said, "you shall not cut his hair."

Manoah and his wife had a son whom they called Samson, and Samson grew up tall and strong and they did not cut his hair. And when he was a grown man he went to a town called Timnath and he saw a daughter of a Philistine with whom he fell in love and wanted to marry.

At first his parents said "No," because they wanted him to marry one of his own people. They did not know that this marriage was part of the Lord's plans to destroy the Philistines, but when Samson insisted they agreed.

So Samson went to Timnath with his parents. As he came to the vineyards a young lion tried to attack him and he killed it with his bare hands, but he did not tell his father and mother what he had done. They continued and he met the Philistine girl and he knew he loved her deeply.

On the way home he passed the place where the lion's body should have been but instead there was a swarm of bees and honey. He took out a handful of honey and ate it and gave some to his parents, but he did not tell them of its strange appearance where the body of the lion should have been.

SAMSON'S RIDDLE

JUDGES 13-14

The marriage of Samson and the lovely Philistine girl was planned and a wedding feast was prepared. There were thirty young Philistine men at the feast and Samson said to them, "Here is a riddle for you and if you can solve it for me within seven days then I shall give you thirty suits of clothes, but if you fail to find the answer you must give me thirty changes of clothing." So they said, "Tell us your riddle."

Samson told them, "Out of the eater came forth meat, and out of the strong came forth sweetness."

Three days passed and the Philistines had found no answer to the riddle. On the seventh day they said to Samson's wife, "See if you can get your husband to tell us the answer or we will set fire to your father's house and burn you alive."

Samson's wife wept and said to him, "You must hate me instead of loving me for you have given my people a riddle to solve and have not told me the answer to it."

"Neither have I told my parents," said Samson.

His wife wept for seven days and all the time the feast was going on. At last on the seventh day Samson could bear it no longer and he told her the answer and she told her people.

Before sunset on the seventh day, the men of the city said to Samson, "What is sweeter than honey, and what is stronger than a lion?"

His wife told him then what had happened. "You would never have known the answer to my riddle if you had not threatened my wife," he said. Then he went down to Ashkelon and there he killed thirty men and took their clothes and he gave these clothes to the men who had answered his riddle. Then he went back to his father's house, terribly angry with his wife and the Philistines.

SAMSON'S ANGER

Samson caught three hundred foxes and tied them tail to tail and fixed torches between their tails. Then he set fire to the torches and let the foxes run through the cornfields of the Philistines so that all the corn and all the vineyards caught fire and burned up. The Philistines then moved their camps closer to Samson and told the people near there, "We have come to capture Samson."

Three thousand men went up to the top of the rock Etam and said to Samson, "The Philistines will kill us all because of you. We are going to bind you and turn you over to them!"

Samson said, "Promise me that you yourselves won't attack me."

"No," they said, "but we will tie you hand and foot. And we will hand you to them."

So they bound him with two new pieces of rope and took him to where the Philistines were. But the Spirit of the Lord descended upon Samson and the ropes became soft and fell from him. He looked around and saw a clean white bone of a donkey and with it he killed a thousand men!

Then he threw away the bone and asked the Lord for only one thing, a drink of water, for there was none to be had and he was parched with thirst. God touched a place in the rock and water gushed out of it and Samson drank his fill until his strength returned.

After that he became a judge in Israel under the Philistines and he judged the people for twenty years.

SAMSON'S STRENGTH

JUDGES 16

Samson fell in love with a woman named Delilah. The leaders of the Philistines came to her and said, "Find out from him where he gets his great strength and we will give you, each of us, eleven hundred pieces of silver."

So Delilah said to Samson, "Tell me, I beg you, what gives you your great strength?"

"If I was bound with seven green willow stems that had never been dried I should be as weak as any other man," Samson told her.

The leaders of the Philistines brought her seven green willow stems that had not been dried and she bound him with them. And the men were hiding in her room and she said to Samson, "The Philistines are going to kill you, Samson!"

Samson broke the stems as if they were bits of string. So the secret of his strength was still not known.

Then Delilah said to Samson, "You have lied to me. Tell me, I beg you, what would really securely bind you?"

And he said, "New ropes that have never been used. Then I shall be as weak as any other man."

Delilah took new ropes and tied him up and said to him, "The Philistines are going to kill you, Samson!"

And again the men were hiding in the room but Samson broke the ropes again as though they were pieces of thread.

"You still tell me lies," Delilah said. "Tell me the truth."

"Weave the seven locks of my hair with the web of cloth on your loom," he said. She did it while he was sleeping and fastened it with the pin of her loom. Then she said, "The Philistines are going to kill you, Samson!" But when he woke he pulled away from the pin of the loom and the web of the cloth.

THE SECRET

"How can you claim to love me when you tell me lies three times?" Delilah said to him. And she scolded him every day. And he loved Delilah very much and it upset him to see her unhappy. So finally he told her his secret.

"I have never cut my hair," he said to her, "for I have been dedicated to God since I was born. If my head was shaved my strength would go from me and I would become weak and like any other man."

Delilah knew then that this was the real secret and she called the lords of the Philistines and they came up bringing her the money they had promised her.

Delilah made Samson go to sleep and his head was on her knees. Then she called for a man and he shaved off seven locks of Samson's hair. Then she said, "The Philistines are going to kill you, Samson!"

He awoke but he did not know the power of the Lord was gone from him and the Philistines quickly took him and put him in prison.

SAMSON'S REVENGE

But gradually his hair began to grow again and the Philistines did not notice. They had a great festival to celebrate the capture of Samson and they said, "Call Samson out so that he can entertain us."

They brought Samson out of the prison and made fun of him. When they stood him up between two pillars, Samson said to the boy who held him by the hand, "Let me feel the pillars which support the house so that I may lean upon them."

Now the house was filled with all the great leaders of the Philistines. There were about three thousand

men and women on the roof watching while they
were making fun of Samson.

Then Samson called out to the Lord, "O Lord
God, remember me and give me back my strength,
only this once!"

Then Samson took hold of the two middle pillars
upon which the house stood and which held it up.
He held one with his right hand and the other with
his left hand.

Samson said, "Let me die with the Philistines,"
and he bowed himself with all his might and the house
fell upon all the people who were inside. And all of
the people were killed.

RUTH

RUTH, THE FAITHFUL

During the time that the Judges ruled there was a great hunger in the land and a woman named Naomi and her husband and their two sons left their own country and travelled to the country of Moab. There they lived very well and the two sons married Moab women. One girl was named Orpah and the other Ruth.

Orpah and Ruth lived happily with their husbands for ten years, and then their husbands died, as did Naomi's husband, and so Naomi decided that she would return to her own people.

"Go," she told her daughters-in-law. "Return to your own homes and pray to your own gods, and may you each find the happiness you gave my sons."

But Ruth refused to leave Naomi, and so she and Naomi returned together to Beth-lehem for the time of the spring harvest.

RUTH MEETS BOAZ

Naomi had a wealthy kinsman, the brother of her dead husband, and his name was Boaz. Ruth went to work in the cornfields that belonged to Boaz. One day Boaz came into the cornfields and he saw Ruth. "Who is that?" he asked his servants.

"That is Ruth, the widow, and the daughter-in-law of Naomi," they said.

Boaz was much taken by Ruth and he said to her, "Let your eyes remain on your work and not on the young men in the fields and I will see that no one dares harm you."

And Boaz invited her to eat with him and she did and then Ruth left and went back to the city to tell Naomi about her meeting with Boaz. Naomi was pleased and bid Ruth to do as Boaz said.

So Ruth worked in the fields for Boaz, doing as he had told her, and each night she returned to the city where she lived with Naomi.

NAOMI TELLS RUTH WHAT TO DO

At the end of the wheat harvest Naomi said to Ruth, "My daughter, you must now find rest and a new life. Boaz is good and wealthy and he is a kinsman. Tonight he shall be in the threshing room where they separate the corn from the stalks. He will work and eat and sleep there and when he is asleep you shall lie down at his feet and when he wakes he will tell you what you shall do."

So Ruth went into the threshing room and hid. Boaz ate and drank until his heart was merry, then he went to sleep at the end of the heap of corn. Then Ruth came softly and laid down at his feet.

At midnight Boaz woke and saw Ruth. "Who are you?" he asked her in the darkness.

"I am Ruth," she said quietly.

"You are blessed," he told her, "for you have not looked at the young men, rich or poor, and you have remained with your mother-in-law, Naomi, and followed your dead husband's faith. All the people of Beth-lehem know you are a good woman. Stay tonight and in the morning I will make arrangements for your future."

Ruth lay at his feet until the morning and then she rose and Boaz said, "Bring your veil to me and hold it out."

When she did so, he placed six measures of barley into the veil. Ruth brought this back to Naomi.

"Wait patiently," Naomi told her. "This man will not rest until you are his wife."

BOAZ BUYS RUTH

That day Boaz met with the rest of Naomi's kinsmen and spoke to the one closest to her.

"Naomi is selling a piece of land which belonged to our brother, her husband," he told him. "I think you should buy it before it goes out of our family. But if you do not wish to, tell me now, so that I can have the next right to buy it, for if you buy the land you must also marry Ruth, the widow of Naomi's son."

"I cannot," the man said. "You can have my rights."

Boaz turned to the others. "You are witnesses that I have bought from Naomi all that belonged to our brother and to his sons and I have bought Ruth to be my wife," he said.

"We are witnesses," they replied, "and may the Lord bless your house and make it famous in Bethlehem."

THE HAPPY ENDING

And Boaz and Ruth were married and Ruth had a little boy, and the women in the town all came to Naomi and said, "Blessed be the name of the Lord, who has not left you without an heir and may he be a famous man when he is grown. He shall surely make you feel young again and care for you in your old age, for he is Ruth's son and she loves you better than seven sons."

And Naomi helped Ruth care for the little boy and the child was called Obed. He became the father of Jesse, who was the father of David.

FIRST BOOK
OF
SAMUEL

THE BIRTH OF SAMUEL

There was a woman named Hannah whose husband, Elkanah, loved her dearly. But Hannah was always sad because she did not have a child. One day she went to the temple of the priest, Eli. She prayed there for a child and she promised that if she had a child she would give him to the Lord to serve Him. Eli, the priest, saw her but he could not hear what she was saying for she was praying silently.

"You shall have what you have prayed for," Eli told her, and Hannah left the temple, no longer sad.

Hannah did have a son and she called him Samuel. And when Samuel no longer needed his mother to feed him, Hannah took him to the temple of Eli.

HANNAH'S SONG OF THANKFULNESS

I SAMUEL 2

"O my Lord, I am the woman
who stood here and prayed before
For this child which You gave to me.
Therefore I bring him to You to serve the Lord
    as long as he lives.
My heart is happy.
My spirit is high.
There is no one other than Our Lord.
There is no rock as strong as You.
We shall not be proud or boastful,
For the Lord has given us whatever we have.
Mighty men are broken,
Weak men given strength.
They who have feasted have starved,
And those who have hungered have been fed.
The Lord gives life and death.
He makes you poor or rich.
He can set the poor among princes
And cause the wicked to lie silent in darkness."

THE SIN OF ELI'S SONS

I SAMUEL 2

Now the sons of Eli, the priest, were not good men and did not believe in the Lord's word. But Samuel grew to be a young boy who followed the Lord. And every year Hannah made him a little coat and brought it to him.

When Eli grew very old he heard about the evil dealings of his own sons and it troubled him greatly.

"I have heard bad reports," he told them. "You must remember if one man sins against the other a judge can judge him, but when he sins against the Lord he can answer only to the Lord."

But Eli's sons would not listen.

GOD CALLS SAMUEL

I SAMUEL 3

As Eli grew old he grew blind and Samuel became his eyes. One night when Eli had gone to sleep, Samuel laid down to rest and he heard the voice of the Lord, but he thought it was Eli calling him and he ran to him.

"I did not call you," Eli said. "Lie down again."

So Samuel again lay down to rest but again he heard a voice call him. Samuel arose and ran to Eli.

"Here I am. You called me," he said.

"I did not, my son," Eli replied. "Lie down again."

When the Lord called Samuel for the third time, Samuel arose and went to Eli but Eli understood that the Lord was calling the boy. Therefore he said, "Go, lie down and when you hear a voice call you again you will say, 'Speak, Lord, and I will listen'."

So Samuel went back to lie in his small bed and the Lord came and stood beside him and called again. This time Samuel stood up.

"Speak, my Lord, and I will listen," he said.

The Lord said to Samuel, "Eli's sons have gone against my word and Eli did not stop them. Therefore, I will judge this house."

Then the Lord went and Samuel lay until morning without sleeping because he was afraid to tell Eli what the Lord had said. But in the morning Eli called him and Samuel arose and went to him.

"What did the Lord say to you?" Eli asked.

And Samuel told him and Eli said, "The Lord God's word is law."

THE ARK IS STOLEN

I SAMUEL 3-4

All Israel knew that the Lord had chosen to speak to Samuel, so Samuel became the man who spoke the Lord's words to the people.

During this time the children of Israel went to war against the Philistines but in their first battle four thousand of their men were killed. They sent messengers to Eli's temple to bring the ark from the temple to the battlefield, which was against the law of the Lord. Eli's two sons were guarding the ark when the messengers came and they let the ark go out of the temple.

When the ark arrived in the camp the men shouted with joy. The Philistines knew the Hebrews had brought the ark to the camp and they were afraid. Still, they attacked the children of Israel. It was a mighty battle and thirty thousand children of Israel were killed. Then the Philistines stole the ark and killed Eli's two sons.

When Eli heard from a tattered soldier about the great slaughter and the death of his sons and the stealing of the ark by the Philistines, the shock was so great and he was so old that he died of a broken heart.

THE PLAGUE OF THE PHILISTINES

I SAMUEL 5

The Philistines brought the ark of God into the temple of Dagon, a false god that was a statue, and set it beside Dagon. When the Philistines arose early the next morning they went straight to the temple of Dagon and found he had fallen to the ground, his face buried in the earth before the ark.

They picked him up and set him back in his place.

The next morning when they returned, Dagon had again fallen to the ground—but this time not only was his face buried in the earth but his hands had been separated from the rest of him.

The priests of Dagon were frightened because they knew the Hand of the Israelites' God was now upon them. So they decided to remove the ark of the God of Israel and send it to another city called Ekron. But the Ekronites cried, "Why have you brought us the ark of the God of Israel? We will all be killed!"

Then they called together all the high lords of the Philistines and said, "Send away the ark of the God of Israel and let it go again to His own temple so that it won't kill us all!"

But the ark remained and the city was struck by a great plague. And the cry of the city went up to heaven.

THE ARK IS RETURNED

I SAMUEL 6

The ark remained with the Philistines for seven months, and the plague continued. Then they went to their priests. "What shall we do?" they asked.

And the priests replied, "Send away the ark and with it an offering."

"What shall the offering be?" the people asked.

"Five golden mice," the priests told them. "Then make a new cart and tie two milk cows to it with no yoke and take the ark of the Lord and lay it upon the cart and put the golden mice in a box by its side and send it away with the cows to lead it."

The Philistines did this and the cows took a straight path, turning neither left nor right, to the border of Beth-shemesh. The farmers of Beth-shemesh were reaping their wheat and they looked up and saw the ark and they rejoiced at seeing it! But they opened the box and took out the five golden mice and the men of Beth-shemesh made offerings to them. The Lord made the men of Beth-shemesh suffer mightily because they had looked into the ark and prayed to false gods.

THE END OF THE PHILISTINES

I SAMUEL 7

Samuel said, "Return to the Lord. Serve Him only and He will deliver you from the Philistines."

The people put away all false gods and served the Lord alone and Samuel told them, "I will pray for you to the Lord."

All the people gathered together at Mizpeh and fasted the entire day and said, "We have sinned against the Lord!"

The Philistines heard that the children of Israel were gathered together at Mizpeh and they attacked them, but as the Philistines drew near the Lord thundered, and most of their men were killed and the men of Israel turned away the rest.

The cities they had taken from Israel were returned, and Samuel remained a judge to his people and he travelled from one city to another to judge for them, but he always returned to Ramah, where he lived.

THE PEOPLE WANT A KING

I SAMUEL 8

Samuel was now growing old and his sons were not as good as he, and took bribes as judges so that justice was not always done. The older people of Israel were worried that Samuel would die and so they came to him saying, "Your sons are not as good a judge as you. Give us a king to judge us."

Samuel spoke to the Lord and then told the people, "If you have a king he will take your sons to drive his chariots. He will make himself captain over all of them and make them reap his harvests and fight his wars. He will take your daughters as servants and they will do his work."

Nevertheless, the people still wanted a king over them. "We will have a king over us," they told Samuel. "Then we will be like other nations and our king may judge us and fight our battles."

Samuel told the Lord what the people said.

"Make them a king," the Lord said.

So Samuel told the people, "All of you go back to your own cities."

SAUL AND THE DONKEYS

I SAMUEL 9

There was a man named Kish and he had a son named Saul who was brighter and taller than most of the other children of Israel. One day some donkeys belonging to Kish were lost and Kish sent Saul and a servant to look for them. They travelled a long way and did not find the donkeys, so Saul told the servant, "We shall turn back so that my father will not worry that we are lost as well."

But the servant suggested they go into the nearby city and speak to the man of God who lived there

and perhaps he could tell them which direction they should take.

"A good idea," Saul said. "Come, let us go."

So they went toward the city to find the man of God and as they were going up the hill to the city they saw some young girls drawing water from a well.

"Is the man of God here?" Saul asked.

"He is," they replied, "but be quick, for he will soon leave for the mountain to pray."

They went into the city and met Samuel on his way up the mountain.

Now, the Lord had told Samuel a day before, "Tomorrow at this time I will send a man out of the land of Benjamin and you shall make him captain over my people and he will save them from the Philistines."

When Samuel saw Saul the Lord said to Samuel, "Behold! That is the man. He shall reign over my people."

Saul said to Samuel, "Can you tell me where I can find Samuel?"

"I am Samuel. Go up before me to the mountaintop and eat with me today and tomorrow. I will tell you all that is in your heart, and as for the donkeys that were lost three days ago, they have been found."

Saul ate with Samuel and when they came back into the city he stayed with Samuel in Samuel's house. They arose early the next morning and as they were going down to the end of the city Samuel said to Saul, "Bid your servant walk before us but you stand still so that I can show you the word of God."

SAMUEL'S WORDS TO SAUL

I SAMUEL 10

"The Lord has appointed you captain over all his people. When you leave me today you will find two men by Rachel's tomb on the border of the land of Israel and they will say to you, 'The donkeys you went to look for have been found but your father is now worried about you'. You shall continue on and come to the plain of Tabor and there you will meet three men, one carrying three kids, the second three loaves of bread and the third a bottle of wine. They will greet you and give you two loaves of bread which you shall take. After that you will come to the hill of God where you will also find the garrison of the Philistines. And as you draw near you will meet a group of priests coming down the mountain and they will have a lute, a tambourine, a pipe and a harp and they shall foretell your future."

"The spirit of the Lord will come to you and you shall become another man. And let it be when these signs come to you that you serve God, for God is with you. And then you shall go down to Gilgal and I will be there to meet you seven days later and show you what you are to do next."

And all these signs came to pass that very day, exactly as Samuel told Saul they would.

SAUL IS CHOSEN KING

I SAMUEL 10-13

Then Samuel brought together all the tribes of Israel. But at first Saul could not be found. And when he did appear he stood among the people and he was a head taller than any of them.

Samuel said to all the people, "This is whom the Lord has chosen to be your king."

"God save the king!" the people shouted.

Then Samuel sent the people to their homes and Saul went home as well and with him went a band of men whose hearts God had touched. But there were some who asked, "How shall this man save us?"

But Saul held the peace and became a great king and a very brave soldier and led the children of Israel into many battles against the Philistines. But he began to disobey the word of the Lord and Samuel told him, "The Lord would have kept your kingdom over Israel for ever but now your kingdom will not continue."

JONATHAN AND THE HONEY

I SAMUEL 14

Saul had a son named Jonathan and Jonathan took one of his armour bearers without his father knowing it and went over to the garrison of the Philistines and there they killed twenty Philistines. And the Philistines wanted revenge, but the Lord stopped the battle from taking place.

Saul then said, "Cursed be the man who eats any food until evening," for that was to be the people's sacrifice to the Lord. They went into the woods and there was honey on the ground, but no one tasted it. But Jonathan had not heard his father's curse and so he took the tip of his rod and dipped it into the honey and tasted it.

Then Saul said to Jonathan, "Tell me what you have done."

"I tasted a little honey with the tip of my rod," Jonathan told his father.

"You will surely die," Saul told him.

But Jonathan had recently led great battles against the Philistines and the people said to Saul, "Jonathan shall be saved as he saved Israel."

And the people rescued Jonathan, and Saul fought the enemies on all sides of him.

SAMUEL FINDS DAVID

I SAMUEL 15-16

But Saul began to go against the word of the Lord and when he won a battle he took the sheep and oxen and lambs of the losers, whereas God had told him not to do so. Samuel came to Saul and told him he had done wrong, and they parted with bitter words.

Then the Lord spoke to Samuel, "I have taken the

kingdom away from Saul and provided a new king, one of the sons of Jesse *(who was the son of Obed, who was the son of Ruth)*. Go to Jesse and tell him."

"How can I go?" Samuel asked. "If Saul hears it he will kill me."

"I shall be with you," the Lord said.

So Samuel went to Jesse and he had all seven of his sons passed before Samuel but none of them was the one the Lord had chosen to be king. "Are these *all* your children?" he asked Jesse.

"There is still my youngest son," Jesse told him. "He tends the sheep."

"Bring him here," Samuel told Jesse.

Jesse sent for the boy. He was a handsome lad and the Lord told Samuel, "Arise, for this is he."

And the boy's name was David and Samuel rose up and went home and the spirit of the Lord touched David. But the spirit of the Lord left Saul.

DAVID PLAYS THE HARP

I SAMUEL 16

Saul became ill and his servants came to him and said, "If a man could play the harp beautifully for you, you would get better."

"Find such a man and bring him to me," Saul said.

One of the servants told him, "I remember such a musician. He is the youngest son of Jesse."

Saul then sent messengers to Jesse and said, "Send me David, your son."

And David came to Saul and stood before him and he played and Saul was cured almost from the first note; and he loved David like a son and made him his armour bearer.

DAVID AND GOLIATH

I SAMUEL 17

Now the Philistines gathered their armies and went to battle against Israel, and Saul gathered his army and they pitched their tents. The Philistines stood on the mountain on the other side and there was a valley between them.

Then Goliath, who was over ten feet tall, came out of the camp of the Philistines. He had a helmet of brass upon his head and was armed in a coat of heavy brass and had more brass around his legs and between his shoulders. The staff of his spear was huge and the head of it weighed six hundred pounds, and he carried a shield as well.

He stood looking over the valley and cried to the army of Israel, "Choose a man among you and let him come to fight me. And if he is able to fight me and kill me, then all the Philistines will be your servants. But if I kill him, then you shall be our servants and serve us."

When the men of Israel saw Goliath they were afraid, but David was not.

Saul sent for David and David told Saul, "I will fight Goliath."

"You cannot, for Goliath has been a man of war since his youth and you are still a boy," Saul told him.

But David replied, "While I kept my father's sheep, a lion came and took a lamb from the flock and I went after him and hit him and took the lamb from his mouth. Then I caught him by his beard and hit him again and killed him. If I can kill a lion I can kill Goliath. The Lord saved me from the paw of the lion. He will save me from the hand of this Philistine."

"Go then," Saul told him, "and God be with you."

DAVID FIGHTS GOLIATH

I SAMUEL 17

Saul armed David with his armour and put a helmet of brass upon his head and also armed him with a coat of brass. And David told Saul, "I cannot wear these, for I have never worn armour before," and removed them. Then he took his staff in his hand and chose five smooth stones from the brook and put them in a bag and took his sling and went toward Goliath.

When Goliath saw David he laughed, for David was but an unarmed boy, and he advanced to kill David.

"You come at me with a sword and a spear," David said, "but I come to you in the name of the Lord and the armies of the Lord which you have defied."

Goliath started towards David and David put his hand in his bag and took out a stone and put it in his sling and slung it and struck Goliath on his forehead. Goliath fell dead to the earth.

When the Philistines saw Goliath was dead, they fled.

JONATHAN AND DAVID

I SAMUEL 18

David and Jonathan became as close as two brothers and Jonathan gave David his own robe and his sword and his bow. David did whatever Saul asked of him and behaved wisely, and Saul then made him an officer over the men at war, by whom David was accepted and loved. So much so, that when he came back into the city the women met him, singing his praises and dancing and playing tambourines and other musical instruments. They praised David *more* than they praised Saul and Saul became very jealous of David, because he feared the people would make David king even over himself.

SAUL'S JEALOUSY

I SAMUEL 18

Saul was afraid of David because the Lord was with him and no longer with Saul, so he thought of a plan. "I will give you my eldest daughter, Merab," he said to David, "but you must be very brave and fight the Lord's battles." Saul thought David would then be killed in battle.

David was very humble. "Who am I or my father's family in Israel," he asked, "that I should be son-in-law to the king?"

But Merab loved another, and Saul's younger daughter, Michal, loved David truly and David loved her and they told this to Saul. This pleased Saul very much, for he thought if David loved Michal so much he would try to be even braver against the Philistines and would *surely* be killed. So he said to David, "You shall be my son-in-law!" And then he spoke secretly to his servants and told them to tell David, "The king is pleased with you and all the people love you.

Marry Michal and become the king's son-in-law."

When the servants told David this he replied, "It is not right that a poor man like me of lowly birth should be the king's son-in-law."

The servants told Saul what David had said and Saul told them to tell David this: "The king does not wish any money for his daughter's hand, but instead one hundred Philistines to be killed in battle." For Saul thought David would thus be killed.

But David went out and killed two hundred Philistines in battle and Saul promised him Michal for his wife. Saul knew the Lord was with David and that his daughter, Michal, loved David very much and this made him more afraid, and he began to think of David as the real enemy and not the Philistines.

MICHAL SAVES DAVID'S LIFE

I SAMUEL 19

Then Saul spoke to Jonathan and asked him to kill David, but Jonathan loved David and so he told him, "My father wants to kill you. Therefore be careful until morning and hide so that neither he nor his servants will find you. I will try to talk to my father meanwhile."

And Jonathan told Saul, "Do not commit this sin against David. He has not sinned against you. He put his life in danger and killed the Philistines. You cannot kill David without cause."

Saul told Jonathan, "You are right. By God's name, David shall live."

Then Jonathan told David what Saul had said and David came to Saul. When Saul had his spear in his hand and David played his music, Saul raised the spear and threw it at David. But David moved aside just in time and the spear struck the wall behind him, and David escaped over the wall and to his house.

But Michal knew her father would have David killed that night, so she helped him escape. That night, after he was gone, she placed a statue in David's bed and when Saul sent messengers to David, Michal was there to greet them and said, "David is sick."

But Saul had the bed carried to his throne room and when he saw what Michal had done he asked her, "Why have you deceived me and let my enemy escape?"

"Because he would have killed me otherwise," Michal lied.

David, meantime, had reached Samuel in Ramah and told him what Saul had tried to do.

DAVID AND JONATHAN PART

I SAMUEL 20

David made his way back again to see Jonathan. "What have I done," he asked him, "that your father should want to kill me?"

"He is envious of your fame," Jonathan told him. "But nothing will happen to you. My father loves me as I love you and he will tell me if he has a plan to kill you."

"Yes, that is so, but as the Lord lives, there is just one small step between me and death!"

"If my father plans an evil deed I shall tell you. Still, tomorrow is the new moon. You shall stay three days by the stone Ezel and I will come and shoot three arrows on its side for a mark. Then, I will say to my boy-servant, 'The arrows are on the side of the stone. Go find them.' Then you will know you are safe. But if I say, 'The arrows are *beyond* the stone,' go away, David, because you will be in danger."

So David hid in a field and the new moon came out. He hid for three days in this place and Jonathan spoke to his father and pleaded for David's life.

Saul grew very angry. "Don't you know that as long as David lives you shall never be king after me?"

"I do not wish to be king if it means David's murder," Jonathan told his father.

Saul grew angrier at this and he hurled his sword at Jonathan, just missing him. And Jonathan rose from the table in fierce anger and left his father's house. He waited until the third morning and then took his boy-servant and his bow and went to the field near the stone Ezel and shot three arrows into the side. But as the lad went to fetch them, he shot another arrow and then called out loudly, "*The arrow is beyond you!*" The lad gathered the arrows and came back and Jonathan sent him back to the city.

But as soon as the lad was gone, David came out of his hiding-place and Jonathan and David embraced. Then David went his way and Jonathan returned to the city.

DAVID SPARES SAUL'S LIFE

I SAMUEL 23-25

And David went to stay with the priests of Nob and Saul followed him and killed the priests. Then many of the people joined with David. When the

Philistines attacked a city, David and his band of men would fight them. One city he saved was the city of Keilah. And when Saul heard David was in that city he gathered his men to attack his own city to kill David.

But David heard that Saul was coming to Keilah and so he took his band of six hundred men from the city and travelled into the wilderness in the mountains of Ziph where Saul could not find him.

But Saul learned that David had moved from the mountains of Ziph to the caves of Engedi, and he took three thousand men with him to find him.

Saul came to the caves and, weary from travel, went inside one and lay down to rest. And David found him there. David lifted his sword to strike Saul but he could not kill this man who was his king and his sword only tore away part of Saul's robe.

Saul woke and saw David who stooped to the ground, saying, "My lord, the king!" Then he rose. "How could you think I would harm you?" he asked. "Just now I raised my sword but I could not kill you and only tore your robe with my blade. For you were chosen king by the Lord and I could never raise my hand against you."

When Saul heard these words and looked at David, he wept. "You are more righteous than I, for you have rewarded me with good and I have rewarded you with evil. Now, behold, I know you will surely be king and that the kingdom of Israel shall be yours. But swear before me, by the Lord, that my name will not be destroyed!"

David swore this to Saul and then Saul went home.

ABIGAIL

I SAMUEL 25

Samuel died and David arose and went down to the wilderness of Paran where he met a wealthy man named Nabal whose wife's name was Abigail. Abigail was good and kind, but Nabal was mean and evil.

David sent messengers to Nabal offering help to shear his sheep, but Nabal sent them away without even feeding them. When Abigail heard this she took two hundred loaves of bread and wine and meat and parched corn and two hundred fig cakes and loaded her donkeys with these gifts. She told her servants to take them to David and his men, but she did not tell her husband. And she rode with them. As she rode towards David, his men came down towards her.

When Abigail saw David she got off her donkey and bowed to him. Then she said, "My lord, hear me out. Do not regard my husband badly. I did not know your men had come to serve him or I would have made them welcome. Let there be no blood shed because of me."

"Blessed are you," said David. "We were on our way to kill Nabal and you have stopped us." Then he took her hand. "Go in peace," he said. "I have listened to you and will not harm Nabal."

So Abigail returned to Nabal and told him what she had done. He held a feast and drank and ate until dawn. He feasted so that he grew sick and died!

Saul had given Michal, his daughter, whom David had first loved, to another man as wife, so when David heard Nabal was dead, he sent messengers to Abigail. "David sent us to you to say he wishes to marry you," they told her.

Abigail arose and bowed and taking five hand-maidens with her, went to meet David. And there, in the wilderness, Abigail became his wife.

SECOND BOOK
OF
SAMUEL

DAVID HEARS OF SAUL'S DEATH

II SAMUEL I

Saul had continued to fight the Philistines. One day a young man came out of Saul's camp with his clothes torn and came to David and fell before him to the ground.

"Where have you come from?" David asked.

"I have escaped from Saul's camp," the young man replied.

"What happened there?" David asked.

"There was a terrible battle and those who did not die, fled. And Saul and Jonathan, his son, are also dead."

"How do you know they are dead?"

The young man then told David, "As I happened by chance to come to Mount Gilboa I saw Saul leaning on his spear, more dead than alive. When he saw me he called to me and I went to his side. 'Who are you?' he asked. 'I am an Amalekite' I told him. 'Kill me, for I am in great pain!' he begged. And I killed him, for I knew he could not live long. Then I took the crown that was on his head and the bracelet that was on his arm and have brought them to you."

"And Jonathan?"

"Jonathan fell in battle."

David mourned Saul, for he had been made king of Israel by the Lord; and he mourned Jonathan, for he had been more than his brother.

DAVID'S LAMENT

II SAMUEL 1

How are the mighty fallen!
Tell it not in Gath,
Nor in the streets of Askelon,
Lest the daughters of the Philistines rejoice!

In the mountains of Gilboa
There shall be no rain or dew,
For there the shields of the mighty
Have been cast away!

How are the mighty fallen
In the midst of battle!
O Jonathan! You were slain
On the high mountains of Gilboa!

Your love to me was wonderful,
Passing the love of a woman.
How are the mighty fallen!
And the reasons for wars lost!

DAVID, KING OF JUDAH

II SAMUEL 3

David was made King of Judah and he and his men lived in the cities of Hebron. But Ishbosheth, who was one of Saul's sons, was made king over all Israel, and Abner was his champion who fought for him. There was a long war between Ishbosheth and David, but David grew stronger and stronger and Ishbosheth became weaker and weaker. But in Ishbosheth's house Abner became as strong as Ishbosheth and then Ishbosheth and Abner had a terrible fight and Abner told him, "I will turn this kingdom over to David so he shall rule over Israel and Judah!" And Ishbosheth was now too frightened of Abner to reply.

Then Abner sent messengers to David, saying, "Make a pact with me and I shall bring all Israel under your rule."

And David told him, "I will do so but I ask one thing of you before I will even see you. Bring Michal, Saul's daughter, with you when you come."

Michal was taken from her husband, who went with her for part of the journey and wept when he left her. Then Abner went on to David.

ABNER AND JOAB AT THE GATE

II SAMUEL 3

Abner went to all the tribes of Israel and gathered them together to make a pact with David. But there was a man named Joab whose brother Abner had killed in battle. And while Abner was returning to David after seeing all the tribes, Joab took Abner aside by a gate to speak quietly to him and there struck Abner and killed him to avenge his brother's death.

David mourned Abner's death and he told his men, "A prince, a great man, has fallen this day in Israel and, because of it, this day I am weaker."

DAVID'S JUSTICE

II SAMUEL 4

There were two men in Ishobeth's household who thought they would gain favour with David by killing Ishobeth. They stole into his bedchamber in the middle of the night and killed him. Then they went to David and told him what they had done.

"When a young man once told me, 'Behold, Saul is dead, I have slain him,' thinking to please me, I gave him his death as his reward; how else can I deal with wicked men who would kill a man in his own house, in his own bed?"

And David had the two men led away.

DAVID BECOMES KING OVER ALL ISRAEL

II SAMUEL 5

All the tribes of Israel then came to David and made him king over all Israel. He was then only thirty years old and he reigned for forty years. He took Zion, which became the city of David, and the people built him a house. And he grew great and the Lord was with him.

When the Philistines heard that David was now king they came and spread out in the valleys around Zion.

David asked the Lord, "Shall I fight the Philistines?"

"Yes," said the Lord "I shall deliver them into your hands."

David fought the Philistines and won and he burned all the false idols they left behind when they fled.

A HOUSE FOR GOD

II SAMUEL 7

The Lord spoke to the prophet Nathan, telling him, "I have not lived in any house since I brought the children of Israel out of Egypt but have walked in a tent with all the children of Israel. Now you shall build Me a house of cedar."

Nathan spoke to David, repeating the Lord's words. And David had a house of cedar built for the Lord.

David reigned over all Israel and gave the people his wisdom and judged their sins.

JONATHAN'S SON

II SAMUEL 9

(Jonathan had a son who was five years old when Jonathan was killed. The child's nurse ran away with Jonathan's son to save him from the Philistines. But while she was running she fell, and the boy, whose name was Mephiboseth, was injured and the boy was thereafter lame.)

David asked of the people, "Is there yet any left of the house of Saul that I may show him kindness for Jonathan's sake?"

There was a servant named Ziba. And Ziba told David, "Jonathan had a son who is lame."

"Where is he?" David asked.

Ziba told him and David sent for Mephiboseth. And when Jonathan's son came before David, he bowed to the floor.

"Do not be afraid," David told him. "I will be kind to you for I loved your father and will give you back all the land that was his and his father's, and you shall stay with me."

So Mephiboseth stayed with David and ate always at his table.

DAVID AND BATHSHEBA

One evening David awoke and walked upon the roof of the palace and from the roof he saw a woman washing herself, and she was very beautiful.

David asked about the woman and found that she was Bathsheba, the wife of Uriah. He sent messengers to her and she came to see him. David knew that he loved Bathsheba, so he sent for Joab to put Uriah into the very heat of the next battle. Joab did so and Uriah was killed in battle.

When Bathsheba heard of her husband's death she mourned him. And when the mourning was past, David sent and fetched her to his house and she became his wife and had a son. But the Lord was very displeased with what David had done.

ABSALOM KILLS HIS BROTHER

II SAMUEL 13

David had many children by his three wives and, among them, Absalom was his favourite son. Absalom had a beautiful sister, who was born of the same mother, and her name was Tamar. Amnon, another of David's sons, was jealous of Absalom and, after a time, came to hate his sister Tamar more than he loved her or his father, and he was evil to her and then threw her out of his house. Tamar returned crying to Absalom's house. And Absalom and Amnon had a terrible fight and Amnon was killed.

David's other sons pleaded for Absalom. David knew that Amnon had done wrong to his sister, Tamar. He longed to comfort Absalom because he loved the young man very much. But Absalom was banished from Jerusalem and was gone three years, and David mourned every day that the young man was away.

Joab sent a widow woman to David and she told him a story about her own two sons that was very similar to that which had happened between Absalom and Amnon and then asked David to judge. But David guessed that Joab had sent the woman and put the words in the woman's mouth so that David would see it was unjust for Absalom to remain banished from Jerusalem.

David called Joab and told him, "Bring Absalom back to Jerusalem and tell him he may live in his own house, but he is never to see or speak to me."

So Absalom was brought home by Joab, but he did not see or speak to David.

JOAB AND ABSALOM

But in all Israel there was not a young man more handsome than Absalom. He was perfect, from the crown of his head to the soles of his feet. Still, Absalom lived in Jerusalem for two years and David did not set eyes upon him.

Absalom was longing to see his father, so he sent messengers to Joab but Joab refused to come. Again he sent messengers and still Joab refused to come to Absalom so Absalom had his servants set fire to Joab's barley field and Joab came to Absalom saying, "Why have your servants set my field on fire?"

"So that you would come to me and then I could ask you to beg my father to see me."

Joab went to David and spoke a second time for Absalom. Then Joab called Absalom and Absalom came to his father and bowed himself to the ground before him. David then told his son to rise and looked at his handsome face and kissed him.

DAVID MOURNS HIS SON

II SAMUEL 16

Soon all Israel came to David for judgment, but saw Absalom. They grew to love him dearly, for his judgments were always fair.

Then one day Absalom came to David and told him, "I made a vow when I was banished from Jerusalem that I would serve the Lord. Now that I have been reconciled with you, I want to keep that vow."

"Go in peace," David told him.

But Absalom went out in battle for the Lord and did many things that were not right. He turned some of the people against his father and then joined the enemy and soon there was a great war.

David wanted to go to battle but the people told him, "Do not go. You are worth ten thousand of us; it is better if you stay in the city."

"What the people feel is best I shall do," David replied. So he stood by the gate of the city and the people came out by the hundreds and by the thousands and David commanded Joab, "Deal gently for my sake with the young man Absalom!" And all the people heard this order about Absalom.

Then the people fought a terrible battle with the enemy and many of those who fought were killed but the Israelites won and Absalom fled from them on the back of a mule. The mule went under the thick boughs of a great oak and Absalom's head was caught and he was lifted from the back of the mule and hung there.

A soldier saw this and went to Joab and told him. Joab said to the man, "Why did you not kill him, for he is our enemy?"

"The king commanded that none should touch the young man, Absalom," the soldier said. "I heard him."

But Joab went to where Absalom was caught and he shot an arrow and killed him. Then he blew his trumpet and the people who were left came and cut Absalom down and buried him there.

Then a messenger was sent to David to tell him his son was dead and the king went to a small chamber and wept, crying: "O my son, Absalom, my son, my son! Absalom! Would God I had died for you! O Absalom, my son, my son!"

KING DAVID AND HIS PEOPLE

II SAMUEL 19

The victory that day was turned into mourning and the people all heard the king's cries and the people were ashamed.

Joab came to the king and said, "It seems to the people that you love your enemies and hate your friends, for if Absalom had lived and your people had all died, it would have pleased you more. You must stop this mourning and comfort your people instead, or worse evil than the loss of the king's son will happen this day."

So the king arose and went to the gate of the city and put away his mourning to comfort his people.

And the people now loved King David even more.

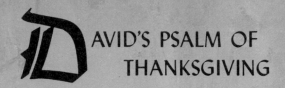AVID'S PSALM OF THANKSGIVING

You are my lamp, O Lord,
And will lighten my darkness.
You are my strength and power,
Your gentleness has made me
   great.

I give thanks to you, O Lord,
And will sing praises to You,
   for evermore.

FIRST BOOK
OF
KINGS

DAVID'S LAST WORDS

David grew very old and remained in his bed. Absalom's younger brother, Adonijah, who was a good man, made himself king without speaking to his father, and many of the people followed him.

But Nathan the prophet and Solomon, Bathsheba's son, did not. So Nathan spoke to Bathsheba, "I will give you counsel," he said, "so that you may save your own life and the life of your son, Solomon. Go to the king's bedchamber and say to him, ' Did you not swear to me that our son Solomon would sit on the throne? Why then does Adonijah reign?' Then I will come into his room while you are still there and tell him this is so."

And so Bathsheba went to the king's bedchamber and bowed to him. "What am I to do for you?" the king asked.

"My lord," Bathsheba said to him, "you swore that our son, Solomon, would reign after you and sit upon your throne, but though you do not know it, another son, Adonijah, is reigning already. If you do not tell the people of Israel who shall sit on your throne before you die, then Solomon and I will be cast out."

Then Nathan entered the bedchamber, "My lord," he said, "have you said Adonijah shall reign after you and sit upon your throne? For he has called the people together but not me or Solomon, and the people have said, 'God save King Adonijah'."

The king was quite angry that Adonijah would do this without telling him first. "Bathsheba," he called.

"Yes, my lord?" Bathsheba said, as she came close to his bedside.

"I will declare to the people today that Solomon shall sit upon my throne in my place," he said to her.

Bathsheba bowed deeply. "I wish the lord King David would live for ever," she told him.

David then told Nathan, "Take my servants and give Solomon my mule and bring him down to Gihon, and there anoint him king over Israel and blow your trumpet and say 'God save King Solomon.' Then bring him here so that he can sit upon my throne and be king in my place."

SOLOMON, THE KING

Nathan did as David charged him and brought Solomon to Gihon and there anointed him and blew a trumpet and called out, "God save King Solomon!"

Then all the people came to Solomon and played on their pipes and rejoiced.

But Adonijah was entertaining at this time and all his guests heard the sound of the people and Joab asked, "What is this noise I hear?"

And he was told, "King David has made Solomon king, and Solomon was brought to his bedside and Solomon bowed to David and our lord King David said, 'God make the name of Solomon greater than my own and make his throne greater than my throne,' and then King David bowed from his bed to Solomon."

All Adonijah's guests were afraid then and rose and every man went his way. Adonijah was also frightened, for he thought Solomon would kill him.

But Solomon said, "If Adonijah remains a worthy man not a hair on his head shall be touched, but if he does evil then he shall die."

Adonijah was then brought before Solomon and Solomon told him to go to his house without fear unless he went against the law of God.

SOLOMON ASKS FOR WISDOM

I KINGS 2-3

Before David died he told Solomon, "Be strong and walk in the Lord God's ways and obey His laws." Then David died and was buried in the city of David.

Then the Lord appeared at night to Solomon in a dream. "Ask what I shall give you," the Lord said.

"O Lord, my God, You have made me king but I am still a boy and know not what to do. Give me, therefore, an understanding heart to judge my people so that I can know good from bad," Solomon said.

The Lord was pleased with Solomon. "Because you have asked for wisdom and not for riches I will be with you and you shall have a wise and understanding heart, and though you have not asked you shall also have riches and honour and there will be no king like you while you live."

SOLOMON'S JUDGMENT

I KINGS 4-5

Two women came before King Solomon and one woman told him, "I live in a house with this woman you see beside me, and I had a child there and this woman had a child there as well and we were alone with no strangers. Then this woman's child died in the night and she awoke at midnight and took my son and laid her own dead son in his place, and when I awoke I saw the dead child and knew it was not mine."

And the other woman said, "No! The living son is my son! The dead child is her son!"

"Bring me a sword!" the king commanded.

And they brought a sword to the king.

"Divide the living child in two and give half to one woman and half to the other," he said.

But the first woman cried out, "O my lord! Don't harm the child! Give the living child to this woman!"

And the second woman said, "Let it be dead so that neither of us shall have a child!"

Solomon gave the child to the first woman. "Give her the living child," he said. "She is the mother."

And the child and its real mother were reunited and all the people of Israel heard of the judgment and knew the wisdom of God was with Solomon. And all the people from the kingdoms all over the earth came to hear the wisdom of Solomon.

A TEMPLE FOR GOD

I KINGS 6-8

When Solomon had reigned for four years he began to build a temple for the Lord. It was made of stone on the outside and cedar wood on the inside and all the work was done away from the building site so that there would be no noise. Then Solomon had an altar built completely covered in pure gold. All the doors were of gold. Two Angels, fifteen feet high, with wings that touched the ceiling, were covered in pure gold as well.

It took seven years for the temple to be built. Then Solomon had all his father's things, which had been dedicated to the Lord, brought into the temple. He called together the older members of the children of Israel and all the heads of the tribes and they brought in the ark of the Lord and placed it under the wings of the Angels. Inside the ark were the two tablets of stone that the Lord had given Moses.

Then Solomon blessed all the people. "Blessed be the Lord God of Israel. I have built a house for the Lord and have placed the ark which holds the Lord's laws in it inside this house. For the Lord God has not failed one promise which He made to Moses. And may all the people on the earth know that the Lord *is* God and that there is none other."

There was then a great feast which lasted seven days. On the eighth day Solomon sent the people away and they blessed him and went to their tents joyful and glad of heart for the goodness that Solomon had done and that the Lord God had done for Solomon and his people.

THE QUEEN OF SHEBA

I KINGS 10

Solomon married the Pharaoh's daughter and he built her a beautiful house. He made peace with all the neighbouring countries and brought all these strangers into Israel. His fame spread very far; as far as to the Queen of Sheba. When she heard of Solomon's wisdom she came from her country to see him and find out if, indeed, he was so wise.

She came to Jerusalem with very many attendants, with camels that bore spices and very much gold and precious stones. She went straight to Solomon to ask him questions, but Solomon already knew the questions she would ask and he told her all that was in her heart. When the Queen of Sheba heard this and saw the temple that Solomon had built she knew he walked with God and was truly wise.

Then she ate with the king. "I did not believe you were wise," she told Solomon, "until I came here and saw for myself. Now I believe you are twice as wise as any report I received concerning your wisdom. Bless the Lord for placing you on the throne of Israel to carry out fair justice."

Then she gave the king much gold and spices and precious stones. Never before had so many wonderful spices been brought to Israel. And King Solomon gave the Queen of Sheba all she asked for and told her all she wanted to know.

Then the Queen of Sheba departed and afterwards King Solomon made a throne of ivory covered in gold. The throne had six steps and the top of the throne was round and two lions held the throne up and twelve lions stood on each side of the six steps. There was nothing like it in any other kingdom.

So King Solomon exceeded all the kings of the earth for riches and wisdom and all the earth sought him to hear the wisdom which God had put in his heart. When they came they brought him presents. Each year the presents grew in size. And Solomon gave freely to the people so that everyone prospered.

SOLOMON'S WIVES

I KINGS 11-14

King Solomon loved many strange women, together with the daughter of the Pharaoh. This did not please the Lord, for He was sure that they could turn Solomon away to worship their own gods. And Solomon had seven hundred wives, and they turned his heart to their gods. Now, when Solomon grew old he was worshipping his wives' gods and the Lord God grew very angry.

God then commanded Solomon *not* to worship any other god, but Solomon did not heed the Lord God's commandment. "You have not kept your vow," God told Solomon, "but for your father, David, I would take the kingdom from you. But the kingdom will not pass to any of your sons. However, for David's sake, I will give one of your sons the rule of one tribe of the children of Israel."

And when Solomon died God did as He said He would. Solomon was buried in the city of David where his father was buried. Solomon's son, Rehoboam, ruled one tribe, Judah, but Israel was ruled by Jeroboam and there were wars between the two all their days. And when each king died he was succeeded by his son.

There were many kings that followed and Israel was then divided into two parts: the north was the kingdom of Israel and the south was the kingdom of Judah. Ahab was now the king of Israel and his wife was named Jezebel, and Ahab built a temple to a false god and Elijah, the prophet, turned against him.

265

ELIJAH AND THE RAVENS

I KINGS 17

The priest, Elijah, said to Ahab after Ahab had built a temple to a false god, "As the Lord God of Israel lives there shall not be rain or dew in the land!"

Then the Lord God spoke to Elijah, saying, "Go; turn eastward and hide by the brook, Cherith. You shall drink from this brook and I have commanded the ravens to feed you there."

So Elijah went to the brook and drank there and the ravens brought him bread and meat in the morning and bread and meat in the evening. But soon the brook dried up because there had been no rain in the land.

God spoke to Elijah again, "Go to Zarephath and live there. I have commanded a widow there to feed you."

So Elijah went to Zarephath and when he came to the gate of the city a widow was there gathering sticks and Elijah called to her, "Fetch me, I pray you, a little water to drink." And as she was going to do so he called to her again, "Bring me, I pray you, some bread as well."

"I have no bread," she told him. "Only a handful of meal in a barrel and a little oil in a jar."

"Do as I say," Elijah told her. "Make the meal and oil into a small cake for me and then make still more for you and your son for the Lord God will see that the barrel never empties and the jar remains the same until the Lord sends rain to our land."

The widow did as Elijah told her and behold! the barrel did not empty and the jar remained the same!

THE WIDOW'S SON

During the long time Elijah stayed with the widow and her small son the son grew very sick and the widow came to Elijah. "What have I done wrong?" she asked him, "that my son should become so sick? He will surely die."

"Give me your son," Elijah told her. Then he took the child from her arms and carried him up to his own room and laid the child on his own bed. Then he cried to the Lord: "O Lord, my God, have You done this thing? If so, I beg You to make the child well again."

The Lord God heard Elijah and the child grew pink and healthy again. Then Elijah took the child back to his mother and said, "See, your son is well."

"Now I know you are a man of God," she told him, "and that everything you say is the word of God."

ELIJAH MEETS OBADIAH

After many days the Lord came to Elijah. "Go to Ahab and I will send rain on the earth."

So Elijah went on his way to see Ahab.

At this time Ahab had called his governor, Obadiah, to him.

(Now Obadiah feared the Lord and was a good man and when Jezebel ordered all the prophets to be killed, Obadiah had taken one hundred of them and hid them in a cave and fed them bread and water.)

"Go into the country," said Ahab to Obadiah, "and find grass so that our animals will not die."

Obadiah met Elijah on his way. Obadiah fell on his knees. "Are you not my lord Elijah?" he asked.

"I am," Elijah told him. "Now rise and tell Ahab I want to see him."

"He will kill me! He has the whole nation searching for you and they have told him they could not find you. Now if I go to him and say 'Elijah wants to see you' he will come immediately, and if he cannot find you, he will kill me in your stead!"

"I will be where Ahab can find me," Elijah told him.

And Obadiah brought Ahab to see Elijah.

ELIJAH'S SIGN

When Ahab met Elijah he said, "It is you who has caused Israel so much trouble."

"Oh, no! It is you!" Elijah told him. "For you have not followed the Lord but a false god, Baal. Now call all the people of Israel to Mount Carmel and I will show you which is the true God!"

Ahab gathered the people on Mount Carmel and Elijah spoke to them. "I am the only prophet of the Lord still alive but Baal's prophets are four hundred and fifty. Therefore, give us two oxen ready to be cooked. Place one on wood with no fire under it. Then let the prophets of Baal call on their god to make the fire light."

The prophets of Baal cried and leapt up and down from morning till night but the fire did not light.

Then Elijah mocked them. "If Baal is a god," he said, "he must be sleeping or on a journey!"

Elijah then took twelve stones for the twelve tribes of the sons of Jacob. With the stones he made an altar in the name of the Lord. He made a trench around the altar and put the wood in the trench. Then he cut the ox in pieces and laid the pieces on the wood. Then he told the people, "Fill four barrels with water and pour it on the ox and the wood." And the people did that. "Do it a second time," he said. And they did. "And a third," and they did and the water now overflowed the trench.

Then Elijah spoke to God, "Let it be known," he said, "that You are the Lord God of Israel."

And fire then leapt from the damp wood and burnt the meat and licked up all the water that was in the trench and the people fell on their faces and cried, "The Lord *He* is the God!"

Then the skies grew black with clouds and there was a great rain.

A STILL SMALL VOICE

I KINGS 19

Ahab told Jezebel the story of what Elijah had done and Jezebel sent a messenger to Elijah saying, "Let the gods kill me if by this time tomorrow you are not dead!"

When Elijah heard this he went to Beersheba, where he had left his servant, and then continued until he

came into the wilderness. There he lay down under a juniper tree to sleep but an Angel awoke him. "Arise and eat," the Angel told him.

Elijah saw a cake and a jar of water beside him so he ate and drank. Then he went back to sleep. Again the Angel awoke him and said "Arise and eat." And there was yet another jar of water beside him so Elijah ate until he was truly filled. Then he got up and travelled onward for forty days and forty nights to mount Horeb. Once there, he lived in the shelter of a cave.

"What are you doing here?" the Lord asked him.

"I am here because Jezebel seeks to kill me," he told the Lord.

"Go forth, be a man, and stand upon the mountain."

Elijah did so and a great wind blew upon the mountain and smashed the rocks. After the wind there came an earthquake and after the earthquake a fire. Elijah still stood on the mountainside. After the fire there was a still small voice.

"What are you doing here?" the still small voice asked.

"The children of Israel have killed their own prophets. Only I remain and Jezebel wants to kill me," Elijah replied.

"Go to Damascus and appoint Hazael to be king over Syria and then appoint Jehu king over Israel and then appoint Elisha to be prophet after you."

Elijah left and went to Damascus where he did as the Lord said. There he found Elisha working a plough and he appointed Elisha to become prophet after him and then Elisha travelled on with Elijah.

NABOTH'S VINEYARD

Bordering the palace grounds of King Ahab and Jezebel, his wife, was a vineyard owned by a man named Naboth. Ahab wanted this vineyard in which to grow special herbs. He went to Naboth and offered him either a better vineyard or more money than the vineyard was worth. But it was Naboth's inheritance, held in his family for many years, and he refused to sell it to the king.

Ahab was very unhappy because he had had his heart set on the vineyard. When he returned to his palace he went to his room and remained there without caring to eat. Jezebel came to him there.

"Why are you so unhappy?" she asked.

"Because I spoke to Naboth and offered him another vineyard and more money than his vineyard is worth but he won't sell it to me," the king told his wife.

"Are you not king of Israel?" Jezebel chided him. "Arise and eat! I will go and get the vineyard for you!"

Then she left him and set to work to write two letters in Ahab's name and sealed them with Ahab's seal and sent them to two noblemen living in the city. "Proclaim a fast," the letters said, "and bring Naboth before the people. Then let two young men come forward to say to Naboth, 'You spoke against your God and king!' Then carry Naboth out and stone him that he may die!"

The two men did as the letters told them and the people killed Naboth. Then they sent a messenger to Jezebel saying, "Naboth is dead."

When Jezebel heard that Naboth was dead she told Ahab to go to Naboth's vineyard and take it. But God had spoken to Elijah, saying, "Go down to meet Ahab, the king of Israel, in the vineyard of Naboth and speak to him saying, 'The Lord says you have killed and stolen the man's land. You shall die in the same place and way that Naboth did'."

Elijah went to the vineyard and there he saw Ahab. "It seems my enemy has found me!" Ahab said.

Elijah replied, "Because you have done evil in the eyes of the Lord, so evil will come to you. All you have shall be taken away from you and Jezebel shall die as she ordered Naboth to die."

Then Ahab dropped to the earth and begged forgiveness of the Lord. He lay there a long while and neither ate nor drank and then the Lord spoke to Elijah, "Because he has humbled himself I will not bring evil to him during his lifetime." But Jezebel died exactly as she had ordered Naboth to die.

JEHOSHAPHAT'S GOOD REIGN

I KINGS 22

Three years later, Jehoshaphat, the king of Judah, came to see the king of Israel. He asked of the king of Israel, "Is there not a prophet of the Lord here who could tell us the word of the Lord?"

The king of Israel sent for Micaiah. "Shall we go to battle against our enemies?" the king of Israel asked Micaiah.

"Go, the Lord shall be with you," Micaiah told him.

But the king of Israel did not believe Micaiah and had him thrown into prison and fed only upon bread and water until the battle should be fought and he returned unharmed and victorious. He rode with Jehoshaphat into battle against Syria.

"I will disguise myself and put on your robes," the king of Israel said.

Jehoshaphat exchanged robes with the king and the king rode into battle dressed as Jehoshaphat. The king of Syria, however, had issued a command to his men to save no life but the life of the king of Israel. They killed the king thinking it was Jehoshaphat.

Jehoshaphat then made peace and his reign was a good one.

SECOND BOOK OF KINGS

FIRE ON THE MOUNTAIN

II KINGS 1

After the death of Ahab his son, Ahaziah, ruled over Israel. During the early part of his reign he became very sick, and so he sent messengers to the false gods and their prophets to ask if he would recover, but his messengers met Elijah while on their way and Elijah told them, "Because the king sent messengers to false gods he will not rise from his bed."

The messengers went back to the king and told him what Elijah had said, and the king was very angry and sent a captain and fifty men to get Elijah and bring him back. They found Elijah on the top of a mountain and as they approached and called for him to come down, Elijah said, "I am a man of God and God shall send down a fire and consume you!"

As he spoke a fire came down from heaven and the captain and all his men were consumed in it. Still, the king was not satisfied. He sent another captain and fifty more men and they also found Elijah on top of the mountain and ordered him to come down. The fire of God came down a second time and consumed the captain and all fifty of his men. Still the king was not satisfied! He sent another captain and fifty more men, but when this captain came near Elijah he fell to his knees. "O man of the Lord," he said to Elijah, "let these fifty men in my charge be precious in your sight."

And the Angel of the Lord told Elijah, "Go with him. Do not be afraid." Elijah went down the mountain with him and to the king and then Elijah told the king he would die because he did not believe in the Lord, and the king never rose from his bed.

THE CHARIOT OF FIRE

II KINGS 2

Elijah grew very old and he knew his days on earth were numbered, so he took Elisha with him to the place from whence he knew he would go up to heaven.

When they reached the river Jordan Elijah removed his robe and bundled it up and hit the waters with it. When he did, the waters parted and he and Elisha walked to the other side. Elijah then asked Elisha, "Tell me what I can do for you before I am taken away."

"Give me a double portion of your spirit," Elisha asked of him.

"That is a hard thing. Nevertheless, it shall be so," Elijah told him.

Then, behold! There appeared a chariot of fire and horses of fire and Elijah got inside unharmed and a huge wind came up, a whirlwind, and carried Elijah up to the heavens.

Then Elisha took Elijah's robe and went back to the river Jordan and struck the waters with the robe as Elijah had done and they parted for him to return to the city. On his way he met some men and they told him that there was no water and the land was dry and parched.

"Bring me some salt," Elisha told them.

They brought Elisha salt and he poured it into the springs and there was water from that time on. And the land was rich with life.

THE WIDOW AND THE OIL

II KINGS 4

A widow who had been the wife of one of the prophet's sons came to Elisha and she was very upset. "You know I have always followed the word of the Lord and now a man to whom I owe a debt has come to take my two sons to serve him as slaves in payment of the debt. What shall I do?"

"What have you in the house?" asked Elisha.

"Only a pot of oil," she replied.

"Then borrow jars from all your neighbours, as many as you can. Fill one from the pot of oil. Soon all will be filled and the oil will not run out," Elisha told her.

So she went back to her house and did as Elisha told her, and it was as he said. The pot of oil did not empty until all the jars were filled. Afterwards, she came to tell Elisha.

"Now, sell the oil and pay the debt and you will never know debt again," he said, and it happened as Elisha said it would.

A BREATH OF LIFE

II KINGS 4

One day Elisha passed by the home of a wealthy woman who always gave him bread when he passed. This time she went to her husband.

"I believe this man is a man of God," she told him. "Let us give him a small room and place a bed and a table and a stool and a candlestick there so that he can rest with us."

The husband agreed and Elisha rested with them. Then Elisha, knowing she had no child and that her husband was old, called the woman to him. She stood in the doorway. "You shall soon embrace a son," he told her.

"It can't be so," she said.

But she did have a son and when the child was grown into a boy, he fell and injured his head. His father had him carried from the field where he lay injured, to his mother. She had the boy placed on the bed that Elisha had slept in and left him there. Then she asked her husband to get a man and a donkey so that she could find the man of God.

"How will you find him?" the husband asked.

"I shall," she said. Then she saddled a donkey and the servant went with her and they rode as fast as they could to mount Carmel. Elisha saw her coming and told his servant, "This is the woman who took us in and gave us a room and food. Run to her and meet her and ask her if all is well."

The•servant did this and the woman told him that all was well. But when she came to Elisha she lay on the ground, crying. Then Elisha knew she had been so grieved that she did not know what she was saying and he knew also that the boy was ill.

"Take my staff," he told his servant, "and run before us to reach the boy as quickly as you can. Talk to no one and when you reach the boy place my staff on the face of the boy."

The servant ran on ahead and did this, but when he reached the boy the boy was dead. He came back to Elisha and the boy's mother and told them. Elisha reached the house and went straight to the boy's room. He closed the door and then put his mouth upon the boy's mouth and his hands upon the boy's hands and breathed his breath into him and soon the boy was warm with life.

The Elisha rose and paced the room, waiting, and the boy sneezed seven times and opened his eyes!

284

THE LEPER AND THE GOLD

II KINGS 5

285

THE LEPER AND THE GOLD

II KINGS 5

The captain of the armies of Syria was a great and honourable man, but he became ill with leprosy. His wife had a maid who had been taken captive during a war with Israel. She told her mistress about Elisha and that he could cure her husband of his leprosy.

The wife then went to the king of Syria and told him what the maid had said. The king gave her six thousand pieces of gold for her husband to give to whoever could cure him.

When the man arrived, the king of Israel did not know what to do. So he sent the man to Elisha. Elisha told the man to go to the river Jordan and wash himself seven times and he would be cured. But the leper was furious, for he could not believe that the waters of the Jordan would heal him better than his own rivers in Damascus. But his servants spoke to him. "If the prophet asks you to do this," they said, "and you are already here, how can it harm you to do as he says?"

So the man went down and dipped himself seven times into the Jordan and he was cured of his leprosy!

Then he came to Elisha and said, "Now I know there is no God on earth but the God of Israel."

He offered Elisha all the gold he had brought but Elisha refused it. Then the man went on his way. But Elisha's servant had seen the gold and he went after the man and told him that his master, Elisha, had changed his mind, which was a lie. The man gave him the gold. When the servant returned to Elisha, Elisha knew what he had done and he cast him out. And lo! the Syrian's leprosy was now upon Elisha's servant!

THE LITTLE KING

II KINGS 11

There followed many wars in Israel. Many kings died. When one battle was lost and Athaliah, who was then the queen mother, found her son, Ahaziah, had been killed, she herself killed all the other princes in the land so that she could rule. But her daughter took one of Ahaziah's sons and hid him and he was not slain.

The child's name was Jehoash and he was hidden in the Temple of the Lord for six years during which time Athaliah ruled. In the seventh year, the child was brought forward and made the rightful king. The people gathered at the temple and shouted, "God save the king!"

When Queen Athaliah heard the people shout she came to the Temple of the Lord. There she saw the little king and heard the sound of trumpets and the rejoicing of the people and she cried, "Treason! Treason!"

But Jehoida, the priest, told the captains of the people, "Make her leave. Anyone who follows her will be killed."

The men cast the queen out and no one did follow her, and Jehoash was only seven years old when he began to reign.

JEHOASH'S ARROWS

Elisha grew old during Jehoash's reign and when he was on his death-bed he called Jehoash to him.

"Take a bow and arrows," he told him. Jehoash did as Elisha commanded. "Now put your hand on the bow." Jehoash did this. Elisha placed his hands over the king's hands. "Open the window to the east," Elisha said. The king opened the window. "Shoot," Elisha told him.

The king shot and the arrow went through the window. "That is the arrow of the Lord's deliverance," Elisha told him. "You will fight the Syrians until you have won."

Then Elisha joined his fathers.

JOSIAH'S GOOD REIGN

II KINGS 22-24

The little king had many problems and other men took the kingdom from him. There were cruel times until another child became king. His name was Josiah. He was only eight years old when he was crowned king. He grew up to be a very good king and he kept the Lord's laws. He had destroyed all the false gods of the people by the time he was eighteen. Then he held a solemn passover and there had not been such a passover held since the time of Moses and there had been none like Josiah since Moses. Josiah fought many brave battles and was killed fighting for the Lord and the people brought him back to Jerusalem in a chariot and buried him there.

And then other kings ruled and evil came back into the land, and other countries took over Israel. And then Jerusalem fell and was taken.

EZRA
NEHEMIAH
and
ESTHER

THE PERSIAN KING

EZRA 1-6

After a time a king was crowned in Persia and his name was Cyrus. Cyrus believed in the Lord God and in the first year of his rule he made a proclamation throughout all his kingdom: "Thus says the king of Persia: The Lord God of Heaven has charged me to build Him a temple at Jerusalem in Judah. All the Lord God's people who are in my kingdom shall be released to return to Jerusalem and build such a temple. And let these people also have silver and gold and goods and beasts and offerings for the House of God in Jerusalem."

All the children of Israel who were in Persia left and returned to Jerusalem. Within two years they had started the work on a temple to God. But the enemies of Judah did not want to see the temple completed and so they hired men to halt the progress. This went on all through the lifetime of King Cyrus and extended into the reign of the next king of Persia, Darius. But then King Darius made a law forbidding anyone to halt the work on the temple, and so the temple was built and finished in the sixth year of Darius's reign.

And the children of Israel and the priests and the rest of the people who had been captives dedicated the temple with great rejoicing.

THE STORY OF EZRA

Ezra was a man of God and a writer as well. He studied the law of the Lord and the king commanded him to set up magistrates and judges to judge all the people and to teach them many things. But the princes of the land came to Ezra and told him that the people of Israel had taken strangers from other lands for their wives, who turned their husbands away from the Lord God and to their heathen gods.

Ezra then fell on his knees and spread out his hands to the Lord and said, "O my Lord! False gods are now making our land unclean. Give us a wall in Judah and in Jerusalem, O Lord, so that we may keep these false gods out of Israel and Judah."

When Ezra had finished praying and confessing, a very great congregation of men and women and children came to him and they wept with him. But they said when they looked at Ezra, "We have sinned against our God and have taken strange wives, yet there is still hope. We will make a vow and cast out all the wives who worship false idols and the children they have borne. And Ezra, please be with us, for you are a man of courage and a man of the Lord."

REBUILDING THE WALL

NEHEMIAH 1-2

Nehemiah went to the king of Persia and the king saw that Nehemiah was very sad.

"Why are you so unhappy?" he asked him.

"Because the city of Jerusalem, where my own father is buried, lies in waste," Nehemiah replied.

"What can I do for you?" the king asked.

"If it please the king to send me to Jerusalem that I might rebuild it," Nehemiah replied.

"How long shall you take and when will you return?" the king asked.

Nehemiah gave him a time and the king agreed. Then Nehemiah arose in the night and, taking a few men with him and little else, went out through the valley and to the gate and the broken walls of Jerusalem. Then Nehemiah told the people of the king's word and the people rose up to rebuild the wall of the city of Jerusalem.

THE WALL IS REBUILT

NEHEMIAH 3-6

The work was divided among the different men of the different tribes, and it was begun. But the Arabians and the Ammonites heard that the wall was being rebuilt so they plotted to destroy it again. Then Nehemiah divided his men into two parties: half guarded the wall while the others worked and the ones who watched stood with their bows ready. Even the builders had swords by their sides.

For fifty-two days the men did not take off their clothes as they stood watch and rebuilt the wall. Finally, it was whole once again.

THE DEDICATION

NEHEMIAH 7-13

When the wall was rebuilt and the doors put in place and the porters and the singers and the priests had been chosen, Nehemiah appointed his brother, Hanani, ruler of the palace and in charge of Jerusalem because he was a faithful man and feared God.

Nehemiah told the people, "Do not open the gates of Jerusalem while the enemy is close. Shut the doors and bar them; appoint men to watch the wall and guard their own houses."

Now the city was large and the houses had not all been rebuilt. So the officials lived in Jerusalem and the rest of the people cast lots for the houses that remained.

And at the dedication of the wall there was much gladness and singing with cymbals and harps. The sons of the singers gathered together and built villages around Jerusalem and the priests purified the people and the gates and the wall. And then Nehemiah prayed to the Lord to remember him.

THE STORY OF ESTHER

ESTHER 1-10

Ahasuerus, the king of the Persians, ruled one hundred and twenty-seven provinces in India and Ethiopia. He gave a big feast and all his nobles and princes from all the provinces were present. The feast lasted seven days and the palace was magnificently decorated.

At the same time Vashti, the queen, gave a feast for all the women of the royal house. Now, on the seventh day of the king's feast, when he was merry with drink, he called his seven chamberlains and ordered them to fetch Queen Vashti so that he could show off her great beauty to all the nobles and princes. But the queen refused to obey the king's command and the king grew very angry.

Then King Ahasuerus turned to his wise men and asked, "What shall we do with Queen Vashti because she has disobeyed the king's command?"

"If it please the king, let there be a royal commandment and let it be written among the laws of the Persians that Queen Vashti come no more before the

king and let the king give her royal estate to another."

So a proclamation went out to find a beautiful young girl for the king. And officers were appointed in all the provinces to look for this girl.

Now there was a Jew named Mordecai who had raised his dead uncle's daughter, Esther, as if she were his own. She was very beautiful. So when the king's officers brought all the beautiful girls before the king, Esther was among them, and it was Esther who pleased him the most. The king did not know she was a Jewess. He gave her the best rooms and he loved her above all the other women in the palace and he set the royal crown upon her head and made her queen in Vashti's place. Then he made a great feast in Esther's honour. Still Esther did not tell the king, nor did Mordecai, that she was a Jewess.

And it came to pass that a large sum of money was raised by the king's treasuries to destroy all the Jews.

Mordecai sent a messenger to Queen Esther to tell her she should now go to the king and declare herself a Jewess and beg the king to save her people. But Esther was afraid. So Mordecai sent her another message telling her she was foolish to think she would be spared above the rest of the Jews.

Esther sent Mordecai this answer: "Gather together all the Jews in the city and fast for three days and three nights and I and my handmaidens shall fast as well. Then I will go to the king and, if I am to die, then I shall die a Jewess."

On the third day of the fast, Esther put on her royal robes and came before the king on his throne. The king was so moved by her beauty that he came down from his throne with his golden sceptre and said to her, "Whatever you want I will give you."

"I would like you to come to a banquet that I have prepared for you," she said.

And the king came to the banquet and again asked Esther, "What can I do for you? Whatever you want you shall have."

"I want you to come again to a dinner with your servant Haman," she said. *(Haman was the man who was to destroy the Jews.)*

Haman went home and told his wife he had been invited to a dinner Queen Esther was giving and that no other men except the king and himself would be there. He was very pleased. So the king and Haman went to the banquet with Esther the queen. And the king said to her again, "What can I do for you? Whatever you ask you shall have."

"If it please my lord, let my life and the lives of my people be spared because I am a Jewess and I have held my tongue, but now my people have been sold and I, with them, am to be destroyed."

"Who has done this thing?" the king asked.

"Haman," Esther said, looking at him.

And Haman was afraid before the king and queen. And the king rose from the dinner table in fury and then Haman begged Esther that his life be spared. But the king had Haman put to death.

The king struck out the order given by Haman and honoured Mordecai by putting him in Haman's place. And the Jews had light and gladness and joy, and many people of the kingdom who were not Jews became Jews, for Mordecai was next to the king and Esther the queen was beloved by him.

JOB

SATAN TEMPTS JOB

JOB 1

There was a man in the land of Uz whose name was Job and that man was perfect and upright and one who feared God and hated evil, and he had seven sons and three daughters. Now there came a day when the sons of God presented themselves to the Lord and Satan came with them.

"Why do you come here?" the Lord asked Satan.

"Because I believe there is evil in every man," Satan told Him.

"Have you not seen My servant, Job? He is a perfect man and follows good in every way," the Lord told Satan.

"Job has everything," Satan told Him. "Take away some of these things and then see how perfect he is."

Well, one day when Job and his family were feasting, a servant came in from the fields to tell him that his servant had been slain and his animals taken away, and before this servant could even finish, another servant ran in and said, "The fire of God is fallen from the heavens and all you had has been burnt and I alone of all your men escaped!"

And while this man talked there came a great wind from the wilderness and the house fell in on his children. Job arose but the children were dead. He fell down upon the ground and prayed and said, "Naked came I out of my mother's womb, and naked I shall return. The Lord gives and the Lord takes away. Blessed be the name of the Lord."

And so Job was not tempted by Satan.

SATAN TEMPTS A SECOND TIME

JOB 2

Now the sons of God again came to present themselves to the Lord, and Satan came among them and the Lord said to Satan, "Why are you here?"

"Because I believe there is evil in every man," Satan replied.

"Have you not seen how good is My servant, Job? No matters what befalls him he still believes and does not move against Me."

"Ah, skin for skin," Satan said. "His life has not been in danger."

"I will place him in your hands," God said, "so that you can see he is perfect; but save his life."

313

And Satan cursed Job with a terrible illness that caused boils to cover his body. But Job still believed in God and would not go against Him.

Then, after a time when the pain and illness did not stop and three of his friends had come to mourn with him, he could stand it no longer and cursed the day he was born. "Let there be darkness," he cried, "let God's light fade and darkness and shadow and clouds and blackness settle on the earth! And as for the night, let darkness seize it so that there will be no sounds of joy in the night. Let the stars stop shining and the dawn held back!"

His three friends argued with Job and told him all the beauties of God's ways and Job told them the great unhappiness that came with following the path of God. But then God came to Job out of a whirlwind and spoke to him:

"Who is this who curses life without knowledge of what life is? Be a man now, for I will demand answers to questions. Where were you when I laid the foundations of the earth? Who made the morning stars sing and closed the doors of the sea so that there would be earth and water? What causes the light and the darkness? Why were you born? Who causes the rain and the flowers to grow? Who has given man wisdom and understanding in his heart?"

Then Job answered the Lord, "What shall I answer You? Tell me." And then he said, "I know that You can do everything and that no thought can be held from You. I beg You to forgive me."

And the Lord had mercy on Job and made his latter years better than his early ones. He became prosperous again and his wife had seven more sons and three more daughters, and Job lived to a very old age to see his great, great grandchildren. And his life was full and his praise of the Lord great.

PROPHETS

THE FIRST THREE PROPHETS

ISAIAH, JEREMIAH (Lamentations)

and EZEKIEL

The last part of the Old Testament was written by the prophets, the men who preached God's words and who told the people what might happen in the future. The first three of these, ISAIAH, JEREMIAH *(who also wrote the* Lamentations *which mourned the fall of Jerusalem) and* EZEKIEL, *all lived during and just after the fall of Jerusalem, and for the following seventy years when the children of Israel wandered again.*

The people at this time were held together and led onward by these prophets who promised them their return to Jerusalem, the end to their wandering and their wars, and also predicted that a man of God, like Moses, would be born to lead them to bring the Gentiles and the Jews together. Isaiah says it this way:

"But in the end it will come to pass
 That the House of the Lord shall be established
 On the top of the mountains;
 And many people and nations shall come and say,
 'Come, let us go up to the mountain of the Lord,
 And to the House of the God of Jacob,
 And He will teach us His ways
 And we will walk in His paths,
 For the law shall go forth from Zion
 And the word of the Lord from Jerusalem
 And He shall judge among many people.
 And they shall turn their swords into plows
 And their spears into pruning forks.
 Nation shall not lift up a sword against nation.
 And they shall fight no more wars.'"

318

DANIEL

THE FOUR PRINCES

Daniel was born when Jerusalem fell, and his people, the children of Israel, were in exile and wandering again. Nebuchadnezzar, the king of Babylon, had captured the city. Now, he gave an order that some of Israel's young princes should remain. He chose only those who were healthy, handsome and very bright. These princes ate and slept in the king's house. They were to be taught the ways and the language of the king, and at the end of three years they were to be brought before King Nebuchadnezzar.

Daniel was one of these princes. There were three others and their names were Shadrach, Meshach, and Abednego. Of the four boys, the king favoured Daniel the most, so when Daniel told the master of the king's household that he would not eat the king's meat, the man was very worried.

"If the king sees your face paler and thinner than any of the other children in the palace, he will turn his anger on me!" he told Daniel.

"Give us ten days," the four princes said, "and we will show you that we won't become thin and pale without the king's meat. Let us eat only vegetables and give us only water to drink for those ten days," Daniel added.

The master of the household agreed to this and gave the four princes only water to drink and vegetables to eat and after the ten days their faces were rosier and fatter than those of the children who had eaten the king's meat and drunk the king's wine. After that they were never made to eat the meat and so they did not go against the law of the Lord that forbade them to eat such unholy food.

DANIEL TELLS THE KING'S DREAM

DANIEL 2

During the second year of Daniel's captivity, the king had a dream and he awoke, troubled and frightened; but he could not remember the dream once he was awake. He called in all his wise men and astrologers and commanded them to tell him what he had dreamt and what the dream meant.

"If you can tell *us* what you dreamt we will interpret it for you, but no one can tell *you* what the dream *was*," they told him.

The king was angry and he ordered them all to be killed. Now Daniel heard of this order and he asked to see the king and was given an audience.

"Don't kill the wise men and the astrologers," Daniel told the king. "I will tell you what your dream was about for there is a God in Heaven Who reveals secrets. He made your dream known to me so that these innocent men could be saved and so you would know God's wisdom. You saw a great image, and it was so large and so glaring that it was terrible. The head was of gold, the breasts and arms of silver, the belly and thighs of brass, the legs of iron, but the feet were of clay. Then a stone smashed the feet of clay to bits and the rest of the giant statue fell and crumbled into such small pieces that when a wind came they were carried away. But the stone that smashed the statue's clay feet became a great mountain and filled the whole earth." Then Daniel told the king what the dream meant. "You are a king of strength and glory. You *are* the head of gold. But after you there shall be another kingdom, not as good as yours; a third kingdom of brass; and the fourth kingdom shall be as strong as iron, but it shall break into pieces.

And as you saw the feet of clay crumble, so shall that
kingdom crumble and then intermingle with all the
other nations on the earth and so disappear. When
that happens, the God in heaven will set up a kingdom that will stand for ever."

The king then fell to his knees and bowed to Daniel,
for Daniel had told him what he had dreamed. Then
the king made Daniel a great man, gave him many
gifts and made him ruler over a part of the country.
And he also made the three other princes, Shadrach,
Meshach, and Abednego, sit in judgment as wise men.

SHADRACH, MESHACH AND ABEDNEGO

DANIEL 3

SHADRACH, MESHACH AND ABEDNEGO

DANIEL 3

Now the King of Babylon had a great statue ninety feet tall made of gold and he issued a decree that all his people, whenever they heard the sound of certain music, should fall down and worship the golden image and whosoever did not would be thrown into a fiery furnace. But the three princes, Shadrach, Meshach, and Abednego, would not follow the decree and they were brought before the king.

The music was then played for them but they still would not fall to their knees and worship a false god, so the king, in a terrible anger, ordered the fiery furnace to be made seven times hotter than usual and Shadrach, Meshach, and Abednego, with all their clothes on, were thrown into it. But when the king looked into the fire, Shadrach, Meshach, and Abednego were dancing in the flames with a fourth person.

"They are unhurt!" the king exclaimed. "And the son of God is with them!"

Then the three princes came out of the fiery furnace and they *were* unhurt; not one hair was singed on their heads, nor did they have the smell of the fire on their clothes.

Then the king said, "Blessed be the God of Shadrach, Meshach, and Abednego, for He has saved them from a fiery death because they would not worship another god."

Then the king rewarded the three princes and issued another decree that no one should say anything against *their* God.

THE KING'S SECOND DREAM

DANIEL 4

The king dreamed a second dream and again it was so terrible he could not remember it when he awoke so he called for Daniel.

"You dreamed there was a tree in the centre of the earth," Daniel told him. "And it was so tall it touched the heaven and there was enough fruit on it to feed every living thing. Then a holy one came down from heaven and cried, 'Cut down the tree, cut off the branches, shake off the leaves, and scatter the fruit; but leave the stump and the roots, and man's heart shall be changed to that of a beast!" Then Daniel looked troubled. "The dream, O king, is about those who hate you and are your enemies. The tree is you, O king, tall and strong: but your enemies will destroy most of your kingdom. Still, your roots shall remain —but you will live like an animal until after a certain time when you will become strong again. For you will know then that the Lord in the heavens rules, not you."

And it all came to pass as Daniel said it would.

THE WRITING ON THE WALL

DANIEL 5

King Nebuchadnezzar died and his son, Belshazzar, became king; and when he did he held a great feast for one thousand of his lords. He took all the golden goblets that had been in the temple of the Lord and served his guests wine in them and as they drank, lo! the fingers of a man's hand appeared in space and then moved and wrote upon the wall. The king was so frightened that his knees knocked together!

But he could not read what the hand had written and so he called out, "Whoever reads this writing and tells me what it means shall be clothed in scarlet and have a chain of gold about his neck and shall be the third in this kingdom in line of rule."

All the king's wise men came in but they could not read what the hand had written. Then the queen spoke and told the king of Daniel and the king remembered Daniel and had him brought into the great banqueting hall.

This is what Daniel told the king: "O king, the most high God gave your father a kingdom and majesty and glory and honour, and so all nations and people followed him. But when he went against God, all this was taken away from him and he lived like an animal until he knew the high God ruled in the kingdom of men. Now you, his son, have gone against the high God. You have taken holy goblets from His temple and drunk wine from them and you have set up idols of gold and silver and brass and iron and wood and stone, which see not, nor hear, nor know. And to the *true* God who holds your life in His hands, you have given nothing. So this is the writing that was written: *Mene, Mene, Tekel, Upharsin.* And this is what it means: *Mene*, By the order of God your

kingdom is no more. *Tekel:* You have been found wanting. *Upharsin:* Your kingdom has been divided and given half to the Medes and half to the Persians."

The king had Daniel clothed in scarlet and placed a gold chain around his neck and issued a proclamation making him third ruler in the kingdom. But that very same night King Belshazzar was killed and Darius, who was a Mede, became king.

329

DANIEL IN THE LIONS' DEN

DANIEL 6

King Darius was very pleased with Daniel. He made him president over the kingdom of one hundred and twenty princes and all the princes had to come to him for approval. This made them unhappy and they

tried to find some fault with Daniel but they could not. Then they plotted against him. They made a law that they presented to King Darius ordering anyone who asked anything of any god or man except the king for thirty days should be cast into a den of lions.

King Darius signed the order. Daniel knew of the order, but he still went to his house and opened his windows facing the city, and kneeled and prayed and gave thanks to his God, as he always did three times a day.

The princes saw him and went immediately to the king. "Did you not sign an order that anyone who asked anything of any god for thirty days, except yourself, should be thrown into a den of lions?" they asked.

"I did," the king replied.

"Daniel does not respect you, for he prays to his

God three times a day," the princes told the king. When the king heard this he was terribly unhappy and he set his heart on saving Daniel. He thought all day about how to save Daniel. Then when the princes came to him again he told them to send Daniel into the lions' den. Then he told Daniel, "Your God will save you."

The king went to his palace and fasted the whole night and he did not sleep. Very early the next morning the king hurried to the den of the lions. Daniel was there, unharmed. The king was much relieved.

"My God has sent His Angel to shut the lions' mouths so they would not hurt me," Daniel told him.

The king then commanded that Daniel be brought up out of the den. And after that Daniel lived well during the reign of King Darius.

A WARNING FROM THE PROPHETS

HOSEA, JOEL, AMOS and OBADIAH

(There were then four more prophets in the Old Testament who warned the children of Israel of the fall of their nations. These were HOSEA, JOEL, AMOS *and* OBADIAH. *Joel warned the people)* :

"There will come a day of darkness
    and gloom
And a great and strong people
Like the noise of chariots shall
    they leap.
They shall run like mighty men,
They shall climb the wall like
    men of war.
They shall march every one on
    his way
And they shall not break ranks.
They shall attack the city.
They shall climb up upon the
    houses.
They shall enter the windows like
    a thief.
The earth shall quake.
The heavens shall tremble.
The sun and the moon shall
    be dark.
And the stars shall not shine."

JONAH AND THE WHALE

JONAH 1-4

Now the word of the Lord came to Jonah and said to him, "Go to Nineveh and stand up against the people of that great city, for they are going into the paths of wickedness."

But Jonah did not do as the Lord told him; instead he went down to Joppa where he found a ship going to Tarhesh, and he paid his fare and he went aboard and the ship sailed for Tarhesh.

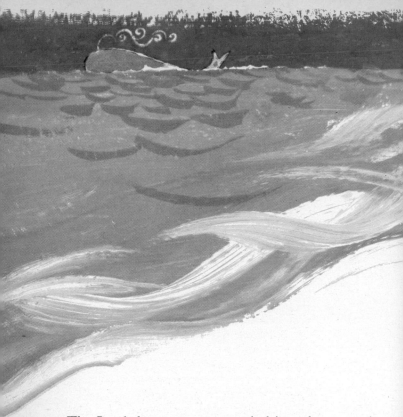

The Lord then sent a great wind into the sea and there was a mighty tempest and the ship was nearly wrecked. All the sailors were afraid and they all cried to their own gods and threw things into the sea from the ship to lighten the load. But Jonah, during this great storm, lay fast asleep down in his cabin.

The master of the ship came to him. "Why are you sleeping?" he asked. "Call on your God to help us, and if He wills it, maybe we will not die."

Then all the sailors gathered. "Come let us cast lots," they said, "so that we will know who it is who caused this terrible thing." So they cast lots and the lot fell upon Jonah.

They came to Jonah. "Tell us," they asked, "where do you come from and what do you do? What is your country? Who are your people?"

"I am a Hebrew," he said, "and I fear the Lord, the God of Heaven who has made the sea and the land." Then he told them what God had asked him to do and how he had gone against His word and come on this ship to Tarhesh.

The men were frightened. "What shall we do to calm the sea that your God has made angry at us?" they asked.

"Take me," Jonah told them, "and throw me into the sea and then the sea shall be calm because I know it is I who has caused this great tempest."

Nevertheless, the men kept Jonah aboard and rowed hard to bring it to shore, but they could not for the sea grew even worse and though they did not want to do so for fear of having a man's death on their conscience, they grew more frightened and so they lifted Jonah and tossed him into the sea. As soon as they had done so the sea became calm again and the men offered the Lord their prayers.

Now the Lord had prepared a giant whale to swallow Jonah and Jonah was in the whale's belly for three days. Jonah prayed to the Lord from the whale's belly and the Lord heard him and spoke to the whale and the whale spat Jonah out of its belly and on to dry land.

Then the word of the Lord came to Jonah the second time, saying, "Go to Nineveh, that great city, and preach what I tell you to preach."

So this time Jonah went to Nineveh and when he got there the first thing he cried to the people was:

"Forty days and Nineveh shall be overthrown!" The people, from the greatest to the smallest, believed him and stopped their wickedness.

God saw what they did and so they were left in peace. Now this displeased Jonah exceedingly and he was very angry and he said to the Lord, "Was not this what I said when I ran from You before? I knew You were a merciful God. Yet You followed me. Therefore, O Lord, take my life, for it is better for me to die than live."

"Do you think you have that right?" the Lord asked.

Jonah could not reply, so he went out of the city and sat on the east side of the city and there he made a small shelter from the sun and sat under it to see what would become of the city. Then God made a giant plant sprout up over the shelter so it was cool inside and Jonah was very glad the plant was there. But by the next morning God had had a worm eat into the plant and the plant withered and died. Then God caused a strong east wind and the sun beat down on Jonah's head until he nearly fainted and *wished* himself dead. Then God said to Jonah, "Do you think you still have the right to be angry?"

"I have the right to be angry until I die," Jonah replied, "when a plant can die so easily."

Then the Lord said, "You have pity on a plant which you did not nurture or make grow and which came up in one night and died in the same time. Then should I not spare Nineveh, that great city with one hundred and twenty thousand people?"

THE PROPHECY

MICAH, NAHUM, HABAKKUK, ZEPHANIAH, HAGGAI, ZECHARIAH
and MALACHI

(After Jonah there were the prophets MICAH, NAHUM, HABAKKUK, ZEPHANIAH, HAGGAI, ZECHARIAH, *and* MALACHI, *and they all preached of a time when all nations would be at peace and worship the Lord in that peace. It is said here by the prophet* ZECHARIAH) :

I lifted up my eyes again and looked
And behold! There was a man with
  a measuring tape in his hand.
"Where are you going?" I asked.
"To measure the city of Jerusalem,"
  he said.
But then an Angel went to meet him.
"Jerusalem shall be a city without
  walls,"
The Angel said, "For the Lord
  will be her wall and glory,
And many nations shall be joined
  to the Lord
And be His people."

And MICAH said:
"The Lord only requires you to
  do just, love mercy, and walk
  humbly with your God."

"BEFORE you weary of the Lord
He will give you a sign.
A virgin shall bear a son
And shall call his name Immanuel.
Butter and honey shall he eat.
That he may know to refuse evil
    and choose good."

ISAIAH.

PROVERBS

1. A wise man will hear, and will increase his learning;
   And a man of understanding shall look for wise counsel.

2. Say not to your neighbour, "Go and come again and tomorrow I will give you," when you have it to give today.

3. The wise shall inherit glory, but shame shall be the portion of fools.

4. Enter not into the path of the wicked, and go not in the way of evil men. Avoid it, pass not by it, turn from it, and pass away.

5. The path of the just is a shining light, the way of the wicked is like darkness; and they know not at what they stumble.

6. A wise son makes a glad father, but a foolish son is the heaviness of his mother.

7. He that hides hatred with lying lips, and he that speaks slander, is a fool.

8. The tongue of the just is silver; the heart of the wicked is worth little.

9. The lips of the righteous feed many, but fools die for want of wisdom.

10. He that troubles his own house shall inherit the wind.

11. Pride goes before destruction and a haughty spirit before a fall.

12. Children's children are the crown of old men; and the glory of children are their fathers.

13. Love not sleep, lest you come to poverty, open your eyes, and you shall be satisfied with bread.

14. A good name is better than great riches, and loving favour better than silver and gold.

15. Train up a child in the way he should go; and when he is old, he will not depart from it.

16. Buy the truth, also wisdom and understanding and sell them not.

17. The locusts have no king, yet they go forth all in a band.

18. The spider takes hold with her hands and lives in kings' palaces.

ECCLESIASTES

1. Vanity of vanities, all is vanity.

2. What profit has a man of all his labour which he takes under the sun?

3. One generation passes away and another generation comes, but the earth stays for ever.

4. The sun also rises, and the sun goes down, and hastens to the place where it arose.

5. The wind goes towards the south and turns about to the north, it whirls about continually, and the wind returns again.

6. All the rivers run into the sea; and yet the sea is not full, for where the rivers come from they return again.

7. The thing that has been is that which shall be, and that which is done is that which shall be done, and there is no new thing under the sun.

8. That which is crooked cannot be made straight; and that which is wanting cannot be numbered.

I said of laughter, It is mad.

I made great works; I build me houses and planted me vineyards:

I made me gardens and orchards, and I planted trees in them of all kind of fruits.

I made me pools of water, to water the wood and make the trees grow.

I got me servants and maidens.

I gathered me silver and gold.

I got me singers and songs.

So I was great.

Then I looked on all the works that my hands had wrought

And on the labour I had done,

And behold! all was vanity and there was no profit under the sun.

Then I saw that the wise man's eyes are in his head; but the fool walks in darkness.

Then I said to my heart, "As it happens to a fool, so it happens to me."

Then I said in my heart, "All this is vanity."

To everything there is a season
And a time to every purpose under the heaven:
A time to be born, and a time to die;
A time to plant, and a time to pluck up that which
is planted;
A time to kill, and a time to heal.
A time to break down, and a time to build up;
A time to weep, and a time to laugh;
A time to mourn, and a time to dance;
A time to cast away stones, and a time to gather
stones together.
A time to embrace, and a time to refrain from
embracing.
A time to get, and a time to lose;
A time to keep, and a time to cast away;
A time to rend, and a time to sew;
A time to keep silence and a time to speak;
A time to love, and a time to hate,
A time of war, and a time of peace.

Two are better than one;
Because they have a good reward for their labour.
For if they fall, the one will lift up his fellow:
But woe to him that is alone when he falls,
For he has not another to help him up.
Again, if two lie together, then they have heat:
But how can one be warm alone?
And if one prevail against him,
Two shall withstand him;
And a threefold cord is not quickly broken.

THE SONG OF SOLOMON

Rise up, my love, my fair one, and come away,
For the winter is past, and the rain is over and
  gone;
The flowers appear on the earth;
The time of the singing of birds is come,
  and the voice of the turtle is heard in our land;
The fig tree puts forth her green figs, and the
Vines with the tender grape give a good smell.
Arise, my love, my fair one, and come away.

Take us the foxes, the little foxes
that spoil the vines; for our vines have tender
  grapes.

BOOK OF
PSALMS

PSALM 3
(A psalm of David when he fled from Absalom, his son.)

Lord, how the numbers of my enemy have grown!
There are so many who have risen up against me.
Many have said of my soul, "There is no help for him
　in God."
But you, O Lord, are a shield to me,
My glory and the reason I lift my head.
I cried to the Lord with my voice
And He heard me from His holy hill.
I laid down and slept,
And I was awakened and the Lord took care of me.
I will not be afraid of ten thousands of people
Even if they surround me.
Arise, O Lord, save me.
O my God, for You have struck all my enemies upon
　the cheek,
And have broken the teeth of the ungodly.
Salvation belongs to the Lord:
Your blessing is upon your people
Amen.

361

PSALM 8

(A psalm of David to the chief musician.)

O Lord, how great is your name in all the earth!
For you have set your glory above the heavens.
Out of the mouths of babes you have sent wisdom
And your might has stilled the enemy.
When I consider your heavens
The work of your fingers,
The moon and the stars you have created
What is man that you are aware of him?
And the son of man that you have visited him?
For you have made him a little lower than the angels
And have crowned him with glory and honour
You made him master of things of your making
And put all things under his feet:
All sheep and oxen, yes, and beasts of the field,
The birds in the air and the fish of the sea.
O Lord, how great is your name on the earth!

PSALM 23

(A psalm of David)

The Lord is my shepherd, I shall not want.
He makes me lie down in green pastures,
He leads me beside the still waters.
He restores my soul:
He leads me in the paths of righteousness for His
    name's sake.
Yes, though I walk through the valley of the shadow
    of death,
I will fear no evil:
For He is with me.
His rod and His staff they comfort me.
He prepares a table before me in the presence of my
    enemies:
He anoints my head with oil; my cup runs over.
Surely goodness and mercy shall follow me all the
    days of my life;
And I will live in the house of the Lord for ever.

PSALM 24

The earth is the Lord's and the fulness thereof,
The world, and they that dwell therein;
For He has founded it upon the seas,
And established it upon the floods.
Lift up your heads,
   And be lifted up,
Open your everlasting doors,
And the King of Glory shall come in.
Who is this King of Glory?
The Lord, strong and mighty,
The Lord of Hosts, He is the King of Glory.

PSALM 67

(A song)

God be merciful to us, and bless us;
And cause His face to shine upon us, amen.
That His way may be known upon earth and nations.
Let the people praise you, O God.
Let all the people praise you.
O let the nations be glad and sing for joy:
For you shall judge the people righteously,
And govern the nations on the earth, amen.
Let the people praise you, O God,
Let all the people praise you.
And God will bless us;
And all the ends of the earth shall fear Him.

PSALM 70
(A psalm of David)

Make haste, O God, to deliver me;
Make haste to help me, O Lord.
Let them be ashamed and confused that seek my soul:
Let them be turned backward and confused who desire
    my hurt.
Let them be turned back for a reward of their shame
    that say, "Aha! Aha!"
Let all those that follow you rejoice, and be glad
And let them say, "Let God be magnified."
But I am poor and needy;
Make haste to help me, O God:
You are my help and my delivery;
O Lord, make haste.

PSALM 100

(A psalm of praise)

Make a joyful noise to the Lord, all the lands.
Serve the Lord with gladness:
Come before His presence with singing.
For the Lord He *is* God:
It is He that has made us, and not we ourselves;
We are His people, and the sheep of His pasture.
Enter into His gates with thanksgiving,
    and into His courts with praise:
Be thankful to Him and bless His name.
For the Lord is good;
His mercy is everlasting;
And His truth endures to all generations.

367

PSALM 108

O God, my heart is fixed;
I will sing and give praise,
Even with my glory.
I will awake early.
I will praise you, O Lord, among the people
And I will sing praises to you among the nations.
For your mercy is great above the heavens:
And your truth reaches to the clouds.
Give us help from trouble:
for vain is the help of man.
Through God we shall do valiantly:
For He it is that shall tread down our enemies.

PSALM 117

O praise the Lord, all you nations;
Praise Him, all you people.
For His merciful kindness is great towards us:
And the truth of the Lord endures for ever.
Praise the Lord.

PSALM 148

Praise the Lord. Praise the Lord from the heavens:
Praise Him in the heights.
Praise Him, sun and moon:
Praise Him, all you stars of light.
Praise Him, you heavens of heavens.
And you waters that are above the heavens.
Let them praise the name of the Lord:
For He commanded, and they were created.
Praise the Lord from the earth and all deeps:
Fire, and hail; snow, and vapours; stormy wind ful-
    filling His word:
Mountains, and all hills; fruitful trees, and all cedars:
Beasts, and all cattle; creeping things, and flying fowl:
Kings of the earth, and all people;
Princes, and all judges of the earth:
Both young men, and maidens; old men and children:
Let them praise the name of the Lord:
For His name alone is excellent;
His glory is above the earth and the heaven.
Praise you the Lord.

"NOT BY
MIGHT
NOR BY
POWER
BUT BY
MY SPIRIT"
THE LORD